INTERNATIONAL SOCIALISM

A quarterly journal of socialist theory

Autumn 1997

Contents

Editorial

Mike Haynes — *Was there a parliamentary alternative in Russia in 1917?* 3

Megan Trudell — *Prelude to revolution: class consciousness and the First World War* 67

Judy Cox — *A light in the darkness* 109

Pete Glatter — *Victor Serge: writing for the future* 117

Gill Hubbard — *A guide to action* 129

Chris Bambery — *Review article: Labour's history of hope and betrayal* 139

Issue 76 of INTERNATIONAL SOCIALISM, quarterly journal of the Socialist Workers Party (Britain)

Published September 1997
Copyright © International Socialism
Distribution/subscriptions: International Socialism,
PO Box 82, London E3.
American distribution: B de Boer, 113 East Center St, Nutley,
New Jersey 07110.
Subscriptions and back copies: PO Box 16085, Chicago
Illinois 60616
Editorial and production: 071-538 1626/071-538 0538
Sales and subscriptions: 071-538 5821
American sales: 773 665 7337

ISBN 1 898876 30 4

Printed by BPCC Wheatons Ltd, Exeter, England
Typeset by East End Offset, London E3
Cover Red Cavalry by Kazimir Malevich 1928/32
Cover design by Sherborne Publications Ltd

For details of back copies see the end pages of this book

Subscription rates for one year (four issues) are:

Britain and overseas (surface):	individual	£14.00 ($30)
	institutional	£25.00
Air speeded supplement:	North America	nil
	Europe/South America	£2.00
	elsewhere	£4.00

Note to contributors
The deadline for articles intended for issue 78 of
International Socialism is 1 December 1997

All contributions should be double-spaced with wide margins.
Please submit two copies. If you write your contribution
using a computer, please also supply a disk, together with
details of the computer and programme used.

INTERNATIONAL SOCIALISM ★

A quarterly journal of socialist theory

RUSSIA'S REVOLUTION has remained intensely controversial for every one of the 80 years since it took place. One central charge made time and again by right wing and liberal critics of the revolution is that the peaceful emergence of a parliamentary regime was frustrated by the Bolshevik revolution of October 1917. Mike Haynes's rebuttal of this argument is unusual in taking the options of Russia's rulers as its starting point. He emphasises the political choices made by the parties of the right and by the socialist supporters of the government. He concludes by demonstrating how these strategies failed to address the most fundamental concerns of the Russian masses and so propelled them towards adopting a revolutionary solution to the crisis.

WAR IS often said to be the midwife of revolution. But it didn't seem that way at the start of the First World War. Then chauvinism and patriotism seemed much more popular among workers than revolutionary socialism. But by the war's end right wing certainties had been shattered. Megan Trudell explains how and why workers' and soldiers' consciousness became so transformed.

A NEWLY PUBLISHED eyewitness account of the Russian Revolution written by British journalist Morgan Philips Price is reviewed by Judy Cox, while the fate of the Russian Revolution is explored in Pete Glatter's review of Victor Serge's *Russia Twenty Years After*. Gill Hubbard examines Paul Le Blanc's restatement of the relevance of the classical Marxist tradition, *From Marx to Gramsci*.

CHRIS BAMBERY provides a framework with which to understand the increasingly speedy disillusionment that many Labour voters feel with Britain's new government in his review of a collection of books on Labour's past.

Was there a parliamentary alternative in Russia in 1917?

MIKE HAYNES

Was the Russian Revolution a mistake? Eighty years on the answer would appear to be yes, not simply for the right but for the victims of the Soviet regime and for its erstwhile supporters in the West. The historian Eric Hobsbawm describes October as a 'freak result of war'. For another penitential ex-Communist it was 'a mistake of truly historic proportions'. But this view depends on two other arguments. The first is that there was a basic continuity between 1917 and what came later. Far from betraying the revolution, as Trotsky claimed, Stalin and his successors in some sense fulfilled it. When the regimes that were created in Eastern Europe by the Red Army after 1945 collapsed and when the Soviet Union itself collapsed in 1991, they therefore carried away with them the whole of the past back to 1917. The second argument is that there was another choice in 1917—that the Bolsheviks and their supporters were wrong to take power as they did and they therefore have primary responsibility for what came after.

Since the first argument is extensively treated elsewhere, our concern here will be with the second one—the rewriting of 1917 itself. Our argument is that the Russian Revolution was an attempt to escape from the bloodiest war that capitalism had yet produced, a war which was creating internal crises everywhere, and which in Russia demanded radical solutions. This war, a product of capitalism at its most barbaric, created a polarisation in Russian society. Workers could either go forward or risk being crushed by chaos and counter-revolution in a way that was subsequently to happen many times in the 20th century. In striking out to overthrow capitalism in Russia the Bolsheviks refused to become 'heroic failures'. Their hope of success, however, depended not only on themselves but on whether the revolution could spread, enabling the Russian Revolution to break out of its isolation. In the event, despite coming close, the hope of a wider revolution was defeated and the revolutionaries in Russia were left isolated. For this isolation the socialist leadership in the West must take primary responsibility for had they taken their opportunities then the result might have been different.

But rather than rehearse familiar arguments to support this analysis, our aim here will be to consider the revolution from another angle and ask why it was that a credible bourgeois democratic alternative could not emerge? Instead of looking at the revolution from the bottom up, from the perspective of the workers, peasants, soldiers and sailors who formed the mass movement, we can explore it from the top down and ask what imperatives led the different sections of the ruling class to act the way they did and what the choices were from their perspective?[1] Only at the end will we return to the agenda of the revolution from below to ask a different question. Why, with clear evidence of support for a soviet-based socialist coalition government without the bourgeoisie, the two other leading socialist parties, the Socialist Revolutionaries and the Mensheviks (and the Menshevik Internationalists), not only refused to support the Bolsheviks but effectively abandoned many of their own supporters in favour of a fruitless attempt to hold out a hand to Russia's ruling class over a now unbridgeable gap. While this decision has won them renewed plaudits from those hostile to the Bolsheviks in 1917 we shall argue that it contributed to the very situation they wished to avoid, namely a weakening of the broad front of the popular movement. Contrary to the many historians who see the Bolsheviks as the only dynamic force after October 1917, the policies that emerged in the first months of the revolution must *in part* be understood in the context of the action and inaction of this part of the left.

Pre-revolutionary Russia

Within the space of a single article it is impossible to review the complex debate on Russian development before 1914 as well as do justice to 1917 itself. We will therefore content ourselves with making three points about how Russian development should be analysed. Firstly, development in Russia was not an autonomous process. It occurred in the context of the deepening and widening of the capitalist system which increasingly tied Russia to the world economy through economic, social, political and military links.

Secondly, this process of capitalist integration created in Russia, as it created elsewhere, structures of uneven and combined development. Development was *uneven* in that different areas of the country, sectors of the economy and sections of society developed at different speeds. Some, at times, showed little sign of change or even moved absolutely backwards. But this does not mean that we can simple counterpose the new to the old, the modern to the traditional, the changing to the unchanging. Development was *combined* in that these forms fed off one another and helped in some ways to mutually reinforce the unevenness of change. A simple but telling example is the link between agriculture and industry. The backward nature of Russian agriculture meant that there was limited demand for agricultural equipment. This held back the development of the Russian agricultural machinery industry in the face of limited demand and foreign competition. Native businessmen in this industry therefore campaigned for protective tariffs and pursued monopolistic practices which kept prices up and so helped to perpetuate the backwardness of the countryside. It was this type of interaction, occurring not only in the economy but across society, that Trotsky was trying to address with his famous concept of 'uneven and combined development'.

Thirdly, when the revolution came it did so in the midst of a world war that was itself a product of the competitive tensions within the wider capitalist system of which Russia was a leading great power. Unless the war is seen as a product of miscalculation or some autonomous political process then both it and Russia's part in it must be seen as expressions of the wider contradictory dynamics of capitalism at the start of the 20th century.

Though in one sense these three points might appear straightforward they nevertheless go against the grain of much recent writing on the origins of the revolution in Russia. This has tended to look at Russia's links to the wider world as an afterthought, is obsessed by the contrasts between the apparent domination of tradition and the few 'islands' of modernity, and introduces the war as an external factor or one which emerges detached from any basis in capitalism in general and Russian capitalism in particular.[2]

By themselves, of course, our three arguments present no more than points of departure for a more detailed analysis of Tsarist Russia that we cannot follow through here. In Russia before 1986 it was common to paint a one-sided and gloomy picture of Tsarist development. Now many have gone to the opposite extreme and see it as a golden age.[3] Since we are primarily interested in the way that the contradictions established before 1914 had an impact in 1917 we will simply draw attention to three more empirical observations about the pattern of development.

Firstly, Tsarist Russia was developing and changing—there was considerable absolute progress without which it is impossible to understand how the revolution became possible. Secondly, this growth was not sufficient to close the relative gap that existed between the Russian economy and those of more advanced capitalism. Despite periods of good growth, the long run growth rate of the Russian economy was not high enough to allow it to close the gap. Whereas in 1870 Russian per capita income was roughly 34 percent of the UK level, by 1910 it was 32 percent—a performance markedly inferior to much of the rest of eastern Europe.[4] Thirdly, although the result of the 1905 Revolution was some political and agrarian reform which it has been argued began to move Russia towards a more liberal democratic path, this argument failed to convince people before 1914. 'No one at the time seriously believed that the autocracy was liberalising,' says a recent historian.[5] Nor has it convinced those who have looked in detail at the patterns of constitutional change, and change in agriculture and the wider economy.

It does not follow from this, however, that we should then agree with those accounts which place so much stress on the extent to which the class structure reflected the continuing weight of tradition that they reject the idea that Tsarist Russia was capitalist. Instead such historians call it feudal or semi-feudal or, like Richard Pipes, define it as a 'patrimonial society' or put it in some other special category—anything which weakens the claim that revolution in 1917 was directed against capitalism.[6]

Such arguments start from two correct observations. The first was well put by the economist and historian Peter Struve, then a Marxist, in the 1890s, that 'the further to the east one goes in Europe, the weaker in politics, the more cowardly, and the baser becomes the bourgeoisie'.[7] Relative economic backwardness meant that a socially weak bourgeoisie had to contest for power with a strong 'old order'. The second was that as Russian society advanced much of it did indeed display an outer shell of tradition. In particular society was formally divided into social estates (*soslovie*) such as those of 'noble', 'merchant', 'peasant' which looked back to society as it existed in the 18th and early 19th centuries. The only national census held in Tsarist Russia used this formal classification, measuring only in a distorted way the real class divisions that were emerging in Russian society at the of the century.[8] Similarly the state administration was divided into uniformed grades, each divided by status, decorations and titles to such an extent that the civil servant obsessed with his position became a stock figure in Russian literature. But we must beware two mistaken developments from these two points.

The first is judging the development of Russia or any other society against some ideal model of 'bourgeois development'—an ideal which has never been able to occur anywhere. The bourgeoisie 'betraying its historical mission' has become such a staple of liberal and left wing historical writing that this idea has become a real hindrance to understanding. It detracts from analysing what actually happened in favour of speculation about 'what should have happened'. The second mistake is then to fail to take into account the variety of forms through which the rule of capital can be expressed. Whereas socialism must depend on the political and economic rule of a self conscious working class for it to have any meaning, the rule of capital is founded at the economic level. It operates more or less effectively through a wide variety of social and political structures. The task of historical analysis is therefore to tease out the ways and extent to which this is taking place.[9]

In fact our knowledge of the complex real history of the ruling class is remarkably sketchy. Too often even its broad contours remain vague. Just as there has been a tendency to reduce the working class to the factory workers and miners (the famous 3.5 million of 1917) ignoring those in transport and distribution, building, small scale production, domestic service, agricultural labour, and seasonal work, as well as the families they had, so too the discussion of the ruling class has tended to reduce it to the study of a few groups. Here we can only alert readers to the danger of this as space will force us too to focus on the broad components of class structure.

Much attention has been paid to the way in which the influence of the industrial bourgeoisie was fractured before 1914.[10] A part of Russian industry was owned by foreign capital. In St Petersburg modern banks and engineering firms dependent on state orders had to a degree come to terms with Tsarism. In Moscow and the Central Industrial Region a textile based bourgeoisie was freeing itself of the traditions of the past and speaking with more independence. So too were businessmen in the south who were based around the mining and iron and steel and in the south west around the sugar industry. But although there was some coming together based on the growing concentration of production and distribution, a question mark still hung over the vigour with which the bourgeoisie could influence the process of change. The liberal theorist and politician Miliukov famously said that it was the professional groups in the *zemstvo* and urban intelligentsia who 'filled the anaemic body of Russian liberalism with red blood [and] gave it at the same time a more advanced and democratic character'.[11]

But a modern bourgeoisie was becoming more articulate and assertive, especially as the economy boomed in the last years before the war. In the *Novoe utro*, the journal of the 'progressive business class', one of their supporters could say just before the war:

Our New Year's toast is raised in honour of the bourgeoisie, the Third Estate of contemporary Russia: to this force which is gaining strength and growing mightily, which thanks to the spiritual and material riches inhering in it, has left far behind the degenerating nobility and the bureaucracy which controls the country's destiny.[12]

We can appreciate this thrust better now as one of the side effects of the collapse of the Soviet regime has been to encourage the publication of studies of Russia's lost private capitalists and millionaires.

However, three other pressures were drawing the different elements of the ruling class closer together even as they disputed for power. The first was the fear of revolt from below. The 1905 Revolution with its urban demonstrations, strikes, soviets, peasant led uprisings in the countryside, and mutinies in the navy quickly confirmed the worst fears not only of the established order but of many just below the top who would have liked to see power move towards them. They therefore began to see clear limits to how they should construct their struggle against Tsarism. As a result it was commonplace on parts of the left to argue that a future Russian revolution would not simply be a bourgeois revolution—even if few were prepared to go as far as Trotsky in his embryonic formulation of the theory of permanent revolution. Outside Russia too, observers like Karl Kautsky reinforced the view that there was a fatal divide between the popular movement and the forces wanting a more modern capitalist society. In his pamphlet *The Driving Forces and Prospects of the Russian Revolution* he argued that:

At the present time the proletariat is no longer a mere appendage and tool of the bourgeoisie, as was the case during bourgeois revolutions, but is an independent class, with independent revolutionary aims. But where the proletariat comes out in this manner, the bourgeoisie ceases to be a revolutionary class. The Russian bourgeoisie, in so far as it is liberal at all and pursues an independent class policy, undoubtedly hates absolutism, but it hates revolution still more... And in so far as it wants political freedom it does so mainly because it regards it as the only means of putting an end to revolution. Thus, the bourgeoisie is not one of the driving forces of the present day revolutionary movement in Russia... The proletariat and the peasantry alone have the firm community of interests during the whole period of the revolutionary struggle. And this is what must serve as the basis of the entire revolutionary tactics of Russian social democracy...[13]

The second pressure pulling the ruling class together was a sense of its imperial mission within Russia. Great Russians made up only 43 percent of the empire's population but their leaders ruled over an empire covering around one sixth of the world's surface. This empire was the result of continual expansion over the centuries. However, in the 19th century pre-capitalist pressures to expand became overlaid by new economic interests and the development of a new sense of Russian 'national identity' as part of the 'nation making process' that was general in Europe at the time. No less in the constituent parts of the empire intellectuals began to develop programmes of 'national independence' which challenged the right of this ruling class to control the destinies of the populations they ruled. This challenge to the destiny of the empire began to bring the old Russia and the new Russia together. In particular those concerned with the economic future of Russia looked to the agriculture of the Ukraine, its coal, iron and steel, the oil of Baku, the cotton of central Asia, while railway and financial interests tied the economy closer together. Liberals were therefore in a dilemma. They opposed the oppressive policies of Tsarism against the national minorities, even to the extent of supporting some autonomy and minority rights, but they cast their arguments within the framework of the continued existence of a greater Russia.[14] Struve, speaking now for conservative liberalism, offered a bridge between the two groups, condemning Ukrainian separatism in particular for the way in which it threatened 'a gigantic and unprecedented schism of the Russian nation, which, such is my deepest conviction, will result in veritable disaster for the state and for the people'.[15]

The third pressure derived from imperialism in the wider sense of a shared interest in ensuring that Russia maintained its position as a great power. Bismarck had said of Russia, 'Let her go eastward. There she is a civilising force.' His hope was that this would reduce tension in Europe and allow the unmolested expansion of German influence in central Europe. But whatever the attraction of exotic internal colonies, Russia's rulers never had any doubt that Russia's 'really vital interests' were in the west, the arena of the main battles with Germany, and for influence in the Balkans and Straits:

> By circumstance, if not by choice, Russia's rank as a Europe Great Power had come in the half-century that had preceded the downfall of the monarchy to depend primarily on her position and strength in the Balkan peninsula. That fact and not Pan-Slavic ideology or the dream of Constantinople dictated the Russian response in the supreme crisis of July 1914.[16]

We can no more cut imperialism out of Russian policy making than we could for any other great power in this period; it was, as its best historian puts it, 'an integral part of the political system in imperial Russia'.[17] It was Struve who again set out the modern logic of Russian imperialism in this wider sense. To sustain itself as a world power Russia's rulers needed external power but this required a powerful and modern internal state.[18] While this led him to argue for reform it also led him to challenge liberalism for being too hostile to the interests of 'Great Russia': 'Russian liberalism will always doom itself to impotence until such time as it acknowledges itself to be Russian and national.' In the end Struve felt that this union was never achieved but we can argue that the war and February Revolution went a long way towards realising just this link.

Indeed when European war came in 1914 Russia played a key role in the crisis, not only in a diplomatic sense but in the way that its conflict with Germany created part of the underlying tension from which the war emerged. In this case, as Norman Stone puts it, 'it was, indeed, the economic "take-off" that men had been predicting for Russia, that…in a sense, caused the First World War since German apprehension of it…led Germany's leaders into provoking a preventative war'.[19]

Caught between war and revolution

Everywhere throughout Europe war brought unity between the ruling class and much of the rest of society. In Russia the central committee of the Cadet party announced: 'Whatever was our relationship to the internal policy of the government, our over-riding duty is to support the one and indivisible fatherland and to preserve its position as one of the great powers, which is now being challenged by the enemy we have. We set aside internal disputes, we will not give them even the slightest cause to hope that our differences will divide us'.[20]

Recent historical research has painted a more positive picture of the performance of the Tsarist armies but this is relative.[21] Everything that can be said about the horrors and strain of war on the Western Front can be said about the Eastern Front and worse. The physical conditions were often more difficult, the trenches shallower on the Russian side, their troops were more badly equipped (lacking not only munitions but even tin hats), the medical backup inadequate, the food supplies worse, and so on. Hindenburg, the German general, recorded how 'sometimes in our battles with the Russians we had to remove the mounds of enemy corpses from before our trenches in order to get a clear field of fire against fresh assaulting waves.' On one estimate in the first ten months of the war alone the Russian armies lost 300,000 men a month, dead, wounded or taken prisoner.[22] On average until the ceasefire in late 1917 Russia's average monthly losses were around 40,000 dead, 120,000 wounded and 60,000 missing or taken prisoner.

The government proved quite unable to create the structure that could sustain this war effort. Into the gap came voluntary organisations headed by liberals but including leading industrial capitalists. The Union of *Zemstvos* headed by Prince G E L'vov played a crucial social role including caring for many of the wounded. Industrial production and war supplies were assisted by the creation of voluntary War Industry Committees. The central organisation was headed by the industrialist A I Guchkov; the Moscow organisation by Pavel Riabushinskii, that in Kiev by the sugar industrialist Mikhail Tereshchenko. Then on 25 August 1915 the Cadets and the Octobrists in the Duma joined with other groups to form the Progressive Bloc to bring pressure on the government to improve the war effort through co-operation with it.

The response of the Tsar and the government was to hold these organisations at arms length. As late as the winter of 1916-1917 the Tsar banned a Moscow conference of the *zemstva*, the role of the War Industries Committees was progressively restricted and on 17 December the Duma was suspended. Even the Tsar's brother could lament as 1916 developed that at the top 'there is no real power, not a shadow of any kind of programme, or desire to understand Russia's actual situation and position in the present troubled days'.[23]

This threw the opposition into a quandary. It is important to understand that although there was a growing belief that the government had to be changed, this was quite different to a commitment to democratisation. In March 1916 Miliukov told the Duma, 'I know that a revolution in Russia will definitely lead us to defeat. If I were told that organising Russia for victory meant organising for revolution I would say, "better leave her as she is, unorganised, for the duration of the war".' But as problems rose it became more difficult to hold this position and Miliukov was forced to make more outspoken attacks. What the leading Cadets wanted was what the newspaper *Rech* called in November 1916 a 'dictatorship enjoying the confidence of the public'.[24]

But if the Tsarist government did not respond to the overtures of the opposition how could it be made to change its views? Guchkov expressed the difficulty well: 'We are almost powerless to struggle with this evil. Our means of struggle is double edged and by encouraging the mood of the popular masses we might put a spark to the fire, the scale of which we can neither foresee or isolate'.[25] Even at the very top Rodzianko, the president of the State Duma, continued to restrain action until the very end. As one recent historian has put it, 'Their aim was not to conduct a thorough social revolution in Russia but to prevent one from developing. They wanted to restructure the political and economic system to provide more opportunities for enterprise, capital and the market.' In the end they waited so long that the matter was taken out of their hands. 'The guilt, if we can speak of the historical guilt of Russian society,' wrote Guchkov, 'consists of this, that Russian society in the form of its leading circles has not been sufficiently aware of the need for this overturn and has not taken it into its own hands, but has allowed blind, elemental forces, moving without a definite plan, to complete this painful operation'.[26] But removing the monarchy proved more than a tidy piece of surgery; it redefined the whole political landscape in Russia.

The trauma of the February Revolution

On 23 February 1917 textile workers in Petrograd inaugurated a wave of strikes and demonstrations which grew daily with control slipping from the authorities. On 27 February the first troops in the city began to go over to the demonstrators and this continued on next day until, on 1 March , the majority of the garrison was in revolt. As news arrived at the military headquarters the now isolated Tsar decided to abdicate. But how would a new government emerge and with what mandate?

On 27 February Rodzianko still refused to allow the Duma to officially reconvene but he was prepared to allow an unofficial meeting which, since it was boycotted by the right, effectively became a meeting of the Progressive Bloc. This elected a Provisional Committee under Rodzianko who was quickly displaced by the Cadet leader Miliukov. At the same time the embryo of the Petrograd Soviet was created. For our purposes the detail of the internal conflicts in the Provisional Committee, between it and the Tsar and between it and the soviet, can be left to the side. Suffice it to say that key figures in the Provisional Committee were anxious to create some form of constitutional monarchy but were prevented from achieving this by more radical members of the Committee and the pressure of the soviet.[27] The soviet leadership saw the revolution as a bourgeois revolution and therefore had no desire to rule but they were determined to be rid of the Romanovs and to ensure that the Provisional Committee upheld a more democratic view of the revolution. The result was not only the abdication of the Tsar and his family but the creation of a Provisional government under Prince L'vov, the *zemstvo* leader, on 1 March with its composition being agreed with the soviet the next day.

The interesting question for us is the nature of the political structure that came out of this February Revolution and to understand this we need to appreciate the extent to which the revolution pulled the political spectrum to the left leaving the idea of 'bourgeois democracy' hanging in the air—precisely the scenario that the liberals had feared before 1917. Just how great this movement was can be seen in the symbols of 1917. The red flag flew everywhere, including over the Tauride Palace where both the Provisional government and the Petrograd Soviet met and over the Winter Palace when Kerensky took up residence there. The holidays institutionalised by the Provisional government were often socialist holidays—most notably May Day. The renaming of things began after February as a symbol of the new era. To be associated with the old order was to be disparaged and threatened and this applied as much to the idea of what was 'bourgeois' as what was 'aristocratic' or 'Tsarist'. On 22 March *Russkoe slovo* lamented: 'Bourgeois. It seems that this word, with its abusive meaning, occupies a position between "scoundrel" and "swine", and its wide usage is explained, apparently, by its polemical convenience.'

We have therefore a paradox. The Provisional government, trying to stabilise a bourgeois democratic system, had problems in even giving this project its name. One contemporary summed it up as 'the fashion for socialism', 'the general aspirations of a huge number of Russians to declare themselves, no matter what, to be socialists, to the amazement of foreigners.' The socialist newspaper *Vpered* in its first issue noted ironically that 'the yellow street press calls itself non-party socialist. The financial newspapers repaint themselves with the protective colour of 'realistic socialism', while the banks try to protect themselves by raising the red banner of revolution over their buildings.'

Alongside the more obvious revolutionary elements, the factory and soldiers committees, the soviets etc, this seismic shift in the political spectrum destabilised political parties and institutions that would normally be the basis of the consolidation of a new order. Even the church was affected. While sections of the hierarchy looked on in horror some turned towards moderate Christian socialism. Still others went further. Vvendenskii, one of the most radical of the clergy, saw no contradiction between Bolshevism and Christianity: 'The struggle on behalf of the poor is the basic principle of socialism, and it is our own Christian struggle.' With these views he was elected to the Petrograd Soviet to represent the 'democratic clergy'. The Orthodox Church even created a special 'Committee on Bolshevism in the Church' as it tried to puzzle out how to deal with the phenomenon.[28]

This created an embarrassing political problem for both the Provisional government and for those who later claimed that the October events represented the imposition of an illegitimate government over a legitimate one. What was the basis of legitimacy of the Provisional government? At one level this produced an apparently bizarre discussion of constitutional theory. More widely, it reflected the ambiguous political legitimacy that the Provisional government had both in respect of the mass of the population and the existing institutions of the state.[29] There was general agreement that a proper constitutional basis of power had to derive from a Constituent Assembly which would create the new constitutional and state structure of a democratic Russia. But until the Constituent Assembly met and deliberated, on what basis could the Provisional government claim to legitimately rule?

There were three possible answers. The most dangerous was that given by Miliukov in a moment of frustration when he stood outside the Tauride Palace on 2 March and someone shouted from the crowd, 'Who elected you?', his reply was 'We were chosen by the Russian Revolution'.[30] But if the Provisional government was chosen by the 'revolution' then what was to stop the 'revolution' getting rid of the Provisional government? Such an idea implicitly thrust the government into the hands of the street, legitimising the role of the soviets and endorsing those leaders who were only too ready to stress the degree to which the Provisional government needed them. Steklov, then editor of the newspaper of the Petrograd Soviet and a member of the Contact Commission set up to liaise between the soviet and the Provisional government, delighted in taunting ministers: 'You must remember that we have only to wish it, and at once you will no longer exist, since you have no independent importance and authority'.[31]

The second solution was to argue that the authority of the Provisional government derived from the old Tsarist Duma. There were, however, two obvious difficulties with this—the first was that the Duma was elected on a narrow basis, entirely unrepresentative of the country.[32] The second was that the Tsar had prorogued the Duma on 27 February in the midst of the crisis. Technically therefore the Duma was not in session to make any decisions at all. The problem was more than a technical one. In the French Revolution the Third Estate resisted the king and declared itself in permanent session gaining the initial stature to turn the Estates General into a National Assembly in the summer of 1789. In Russia the Duma and its leaders meekly obeyed the Tsar's ruling, committing 'suicide', as Miliukov put it, 'without protest'.[33]

This left the third possibility, that the Provisional government might claim legitimacy from the Tsar. Yet constitutionally and politically this was no less satisfactory although in a technical sense this is exactly what happened. The best legal minds of the Cadet Party struggled to make sense of this and to give it an appearance of authority. The difficulty was that in abdicating the Tsar should have allowed the throne to pass to his son under a regent. But, fearing for his son's health and future, he abdicated for him too—something which constitutionally he had no power to do.[34] The throne then 'passed' to the Tsar's brother, the Grand Duke Mikhail, who in turn 'abdicated'. Mikhail did not want to be thought of as having accepted the title of Emperor even for a moment. But the Cadet constitutionalists prevailed on him to 'formally' pass on his 'authority' to the Provisional government to give it some sense of legitimacy. Even Kerensky went along with this pretence of a transfer of power, pretentiously telling the Grand Duke that 'we will carry the precious vessel of your authority to the Constituent Assembly without spilling a single drop'.[35] The constitutional importance of this was, as Nol'de and Nabokov (the two key authors of the constitutional fiction) put it, that the 'act of 3 March was in essence the only constitution during the period of existence of the Provisional government'.[36]

Yet it remained impossible to bind the February Revolution in these constitutional limits.[37] What was necessary was for the Provisional government to maintain a popular base. One way of doing this was to include representatives from below—this was the attraction of the appointment of Kerensky. Shingarov, defending Kerensky's appointment to the first Provisional government, argued, 'we must detach from the revolution one of its leaders... Of them Kerensky is the only one... Much better to have him with you than against you'.[38] Another was to keep confidence by reform. Russia quickly became, as Lenin happily recognised, the freest country in the world. The Provisional government was a reforming government supporting a Constituent Assembly based on universal suffrage; universal suffrage in local elections implemented in 1917; the abolition of racial and religious discrimination; freedom for religion; freedom of speech and assembly; the right to strike; soldiers to be citizens in uniform. But there were limits to how far it could go. Russia remained a class society in which the political possibilities were structured by the conflicting interests of those at the top and those at the bottom of society. The programme of the Provisional government therefore 'was a charter of democratic freedoms, not a programme for the transformation of society'.[39] It was the failure to hold the line at such a charter that would lead to Russia being split apart. To see how this happened we need to explore why it was so difficult for liberal democracy to find a mass base in 1917.

The missing base of bourgeois democracy

To understand the difficulties of creating a stable party political system that might be the agency of capitalist rule it is necessary to explore the pattern of party support in 1917 in some detail. One aspect of this was the initial fragmentation of the party structure. This is not unusual in new democracies but it nevertheless complicated the task of creating a stable political base with more than 100 parties contesting for power.[40] But within this mass of organisations there were half a dozen which were significant on a national scale. Three were on the centre right, the Trade Industrialists, the Union of House Owners, and the Cadets. In 1917, however, it was the Cadets who were the main capitalist party. Cadet ideologists had tried to maintain that it was a liberal supra-class party which could speak 'for Russia'.

Now, in the post-February period, the more conservative Nationalist and Octobrist parties were marginalised by the swing to the left and the Cadets became the home for the centre right. Symptomatic was the decision of the conservative Prince Trubetskoi to join the party after a decade of attacking it for failing to protect the interest of property. Leading figures worked closely with key industrialists like Alexander Konovalov and Mikhail Tereshchenko, with the All Russian Union of Trade and Industry, and with Pavel Riabushinski and Sergei Tretiakov even though some key figures in business continued to dislike the way in which the party looked more positively on state industry and agrarian reform than they did. But the party was increasingly able to draw pro-landlord and pro-business support around it because it was seen as the only viable party for the articulation of the interests of property within the democratic party spectrum.

Within the party the balance of power began to tip away from the left which had been more sympathetic to reform and building links with popular democracy towards a centre right position. 'The party', says Rosenberg, 'was…increasingly regarded by left and right alike as the political core of bourgeois Russia'. The dominance of the centre right was reflected in its capacity to defeat the left by a two to one majority on key issues and then in the effective marginalisation of the more radical Nekrasov and the left. As Kerensky put it, the Cadets now 'organised all the political and social forces of the country representing the interests of the propertied classes, the high command, the remnants of the old bureaucracy, and even fragments of the aristocracy'.[41]

The debate on what the vote for the Constituent Assembly represented for the left depends crucially on whether the Socialist Revolutionary (SR) vote is seen as support for the right and centre SR position of opposition to revolution or for left SR support for revolution and we will take this up later. Here we are interested in another aspect of the results. Table 1 shows that in the elections for the Constituent Assembly in November 1917 the Cadets and others managed to get only 6-7 percent of the vote with a mere 17 representatives out of 700. This in no sense represented a decline in the party's influence—in some respects it was as strong, or stronger at this point than it had been earlier precisely because it was now seen as the alternative on the centre right. It had a membership of some 100,000 and the best financial base of the major parties. Moreover it was undoubtedly the best organised national party in conventional terms. During 1917 it had local organisations throughout Russia that could stand its slate in 80 percent of Russian towns.[42] Why then was the Cadet Party and the centre right more generally so weak in terms of the votes it could attract?

TABLE 1: MAJOR PARTIES IN THE ELECTIONS TO THE CONSTITUENT ASSEMBLY [43]

	Percent vote	Number of seats
ALL-RUSSIAN SOCIALIST PARTIES		
Socialist Revolutionaries	38	299
Left Socialist Revolutionaries	—	39
Bolsheviks	24	168
Mensheviks	3	18
Other socialist	1	4
ALL-RUSSIAN NON-SOCIALIST PARTIES		
Cadet	5	17
Other	1	—
Cossacks	2	9
Christian (various)	0.5	—
MAJOR UKRAINIAN PARTIES AND JOINT LISTS		
Uk Socialist Revolutionaries	6	83
Uk Socialist bloc	9	—
OTHER		
Mohammeden	2	—
Other nationalist	4	66
Unclassified	5	—
TOTAL	100	703

The underlying reason was that Russian business and landed circles had not been able to establish a mass base as they had in the west where they could draw on a growing middle class, a property owning peasantry and a body of working class conservatives to bolster their otherwise small numbers. In the countryside the numbers of landowners, even with their families and hangers on, was small and even if we accept the dubious estimates that there were some 2 million rich peasants and assume that they would be attracted to the centre right that still leaves a very small base. The situation was better in the towns but even here there were problems both in respect of the size of the potential social base and the lack of a tradition of mobilisation of it or indeed a capacity to mobilise it in the direction of the centre right.[44] This problem was then compounded by the radicalising effect of the revolution which pulled the political spectrum even further to the left—for example, in Petrograd even in the Vasilevsky Island district where most

of the university was located and where the Cadets hoped to do especially well they managed to mobilise only 18 percent of the vote in the
spring local elections.

Indeed the analysis of the general urban electoral performance of
Cadets, Trade Industrialists and House Owners shows that everywhere
they made up only a minority force.[45] As Rosenberg, the leading historian of the party, puts it, 'Russia's first elections of the revolutionary
period showed the Cadets with a staggering loss of city influence and
prestige in the two strongest areas of past support.' In Petrograd,
whereas they had got 61 percent of the votes for the first Duma after
the 1905 revolution, in the May 1917 municipal elections they now
got 22 percent. In the Moscow municipal elections they managed only
17 percent compared to 63 percent a decade earlier. 'Socialists over-
whelmed Cadets even in parts of the city that were heavily bourgeois.'
When later local provincial results came through they were just as
bad. In Kursk and Samara where they had won every seat in the first
Duma they had only 17 and 9 percent of the votes respectively.[46] The
pattern of local urban voting reveals what Rosenberg calls 'a remarkable fact...the small success of right wing groups in almost all large
towns...in larger centres dumas fell almost entirely under socialist
control.' In fact, as Rosenberg shows, non-socialist party voting was
inversely related to the size of town with the Cadets doing rather
better in medium sized towns and the Trade Industrialists and House
Owners doing better in the backwater towns of provincial Russia
which were often no more than administrative and market centres.[47]

At no point in 1917, therefore, could unambiguously pro-capitalist
parties have come anywhere near achieving a respectable minority vote in
any electoral test. Their dilemma was echoed by *Russkaya vedomosti* in
July: 'The Cadet organisation has little influence in the present revolutionary moment of our history.' Yet the Cadets were the driving force of
the Provisional government. Thus we can say that the very possibility of
the leading bourgeois democratic party surviving depended on its ability
to limit democracy for fear that it would be swept away. As Rosenberg
put it, 'With their own limited national constituency, the Cadets themselves could never claim to rule on the basis of representative
principles'.[48]

The Constituent Assembly

On 3 March the Provisional government announced the 'immediate
preparation...on the basis of universal, equal, direct and secret ballot' for
a Constituent Assembly 'which will determine the form of government
and the constitution of the country'.[49] But the lack of real commitment to

the Constituent Assembly, especially on the right is often vastly underestimated. Even Kerensky from the outset accepted much of the argument for the delay in the Constituent Assembly.[50] But the most powerful resistance came from the Cadets. Despite the Provisional government's proclamation, the very *next day* Miliukov told the French ambassador that he was trying to avoid the setting of any precise date for elections. Indeed a significant part of the Cadet leadership hoped that elections might be delayed until the end of the war. Behind the arguments of the Cadets was a twofold fear. The first was party political. Until the summer of 1917 the Cadets were transfixed not by the fear of a pro-Bolshevik vote but a massive pro-Socialist Revolutionary vote in the rural areas so that, as Kochan puts it, 'it was a matter of political self-preservation for the Cadets to delay the elections.' From the summer the threat became that of the even more radical Bolsheviks.[51]

This led on to the second fear that with minimal influence the Constituent Assembly would legitimate a radical social revolution in both town and country. Thus to maintain both the role of the party and to stabilise Russia it was necessary to delay the Constituent Assembly as long as possible. Maklakov, one of the founders of the Cadets, told the Duma in May that 'Russia had received in the revolution more freedom than she could manage', while the Cadet paper *Svobodnyi narod* argued that 'the larger part of the dark masses of people simply are not able to understand the present meaning of freedom.' To paraphrase Nabokov, instead of the Constituent Assembly being the basis for the creation of order, the creation of order had to be the basis of the Constituent Assembly.[52]

It is not surprising therefore that it took three weeks to announce the commission to decide the election procedures, that it then took two months for it to complete its nomination process only for it then to become bogged down in wrangling over whether the voting age should be 18, 20 or 21; whether deserters could vote; whether members of the Romanov family could vote, and so on. When the Provisional government announced on 14 June that elections would be held on 17 September it did so only as an explicit attempt to draw the teeth of the near half a million strong pro-Bolshevik demonstration in Petrograd on 18 June. Moreover it only did this despite the opposition of the electoral commission under its Cadet leader Kokoshkin. Miliukov and the Cadet leadership inside and outside of the election committee then tried to delay things further. Significantly Kokoshkin was replaced by Nabokov, another Cadet, who would ideally have liked the elections postponed until the end of the war and who had initially threatened, in the face of the September date, that the Cadets might boycott the Constituent Assembly. Success in further delaying the elections came after the July

Days when part of the price that Miliukov was able to extract for Cadet participation in the second coalition was the postponement of the elections until 12 November, announced on 9 August (in the midst of the build up toward the failed Kornilov coup). Whether elections would have been held then and with what effect had the revolution not have taken place remains an open question.

The imperatives of war

Every account of 1917 stresses the extent to which the continued strain of war contributed more than anything else to the disintegration of Russian society. Chernov, the SR leader, told the first All-Russian Congress of Soviets that 'the war is a great pump which sucks out the strength of the country. Here is the danger, and one all the greater because no one knows if the revolution can live through it.' And looking back Kerensky would say that 'it was precisely the war, and only the war…with all its material and psychological consequences, that provoked the collapse of the democratic government'.[53] Why then did the Provisional government not simply cut its losses and leave the war or even try just to hold the front without engaging in serious military action? Was this the great missed opportunity of 1917?[54]

To argue in this way is to misunderstand completely what was at stake in the war effort and why the major part of the Russian ruling class remained committed to it until the bitter end. The Provisional government certainly would have been happy with a general peace but it did not falter in its commitment to the war. In this it had the whole-hearted support of the majority of those with power in Russian society. 'A separate peace with Germany and Austria was rejected out of hand by every political group…no matter how one sifts the evidence, a general peace appears to have been out of the question in 1917'.[55] As we have seen, participation in the war in 1914 was a direct expression of Russia's imperial interests as a great power. This was then accentuated by the impact of the February Revolution which was 'created by a high enthusiasm of patriotism which flatly refused any thought of the possibility of a separate peace'.[56]

Already early in 1917 the fear was that Russia's problems were leading to it being marginalised in Allied discussions and therefore credibility needed to be restored by even greater efforts. If the point of the February Revolution was to create a more modern Russia then that had to be a 'great power' Russia. There could be and was argument over what this might mean but there was a widespread acceptance that a Russia that withdrew from the war would inevitably have to take second place to whoever won it. The worse case would be a German victory since German capitalism was the immediate threat, but a victory for the Allies without Russia might create as many difficulties in the longer run since it too would imply Russia's subordination. And lest it be thought that this fear was unfounded we should recall that in 1918 when Russia's old rulers were in exile but still hoping they might be restored, Clemenceau brutally dismissed their claims for 'Russian' influence in any post-war settlement: 'Russia is a neutral country which has concluded a separate peace with our enemies. The friends of our enemies are our enemies'.[57]

Then there was the fact that the war was begun ostensibly in a 'Slavonic cause'. Interest in this was heightened by the specific gains that might be made in the Balkans. In theory these were 'guaranteed' by the infamous secret treaties signed to carve up the weaker parts of Europe when the Allies won. In particular Russia would gain Constantinople and the Straits, Galicia, Bukovina, Turkish Armenia and parts of Persia. Rodichev told the seventh Congress of the Cadets, 'Citizens, they say that these are the strivings of Russian imperialism and seizure. No! This is not seizure. It is the foundation of Russian independence.' This line was echoed by Miliukov, 'probably the strongest imperialist in the country', suggested Arthur Ransome. According to Nabokov, Miliukov:

> *...was absolutely alien and hostile to the idea of peace without annexations and indemnities. He considered that it would be absurd and simply criminal of us to renounce the 'greatest prize of the war' (as Grey, the British foreign secretary, called Constantinople and the Straits)... But, most importantly, he believed that this prize had not actually slipped from our grasp.*

These arguments were not aberrations, they reflected what Geyer calls 'the astonishing fixation which both Russian policy makers and the public showed for this region'.[58]

Pressure too came from the army. Leading officers were especially committed to these imperial ideals: 'We reject the very idea that a Free Russia should be denied the free access to the Mediterranean which will ensure the economic well-being of the population, and we consider that the sole guarantee of such freedom of access would be either general disarmament, or, in default of that, military control over the Straits by Russia', said a motion passed at the Congress of Officers in April 1917.[59] But beyond this the generals expected to fight. The aim was to go on the offensive two to three months after February. And if this did not have strategic military justification (and there was widespread belief that it did) then it certainly had justification in terms of morale. Alekseev, commander in chief at the time of the June offensive believed that only an offensive would restore morale. Kerensky echoed this view:

To say to an army in the midst of war that under no circumstances would it be compelled to fight is tantamount to transforming the troops into a meaningless mob, useless, restless, irritable and therefore capable of all sorts of excesses. For this reason, and to preserve the interior of the country from the grave wave of anarchy threatening the front, it was incumbent upon us...to make of it once more an army, ie to bring it back to the psychology of action, or of impending action.[60]

Thirdly there were the wider societal implications of any withdrawal from the war or effective suspension of it. There was concern in the army that peace might encourage further disintegration Even before he resigned as foreign minister, Miliukov told Nabokov, 'Perhaps it is due to the war that everything here is somehow still holding together, and without the war everything would still collapse'.[61] Finally we should note that internally there was still optimism that the war was still winnable. This was especially the view at the centre of the Cadet Party. 'Our party's policy constantly strove to maintain this official optimism,' wrote Nabokov.[62] American entry in particular strengthened this hope.

Beyond these internal factors was the way that Russia was tied to the wider international war effort of the Allies. In allied capitals the February Revolution was welcomed precisely because it seemed to promise more commitment to the war effort. 'It must be remembered' wrote *The Times* somewhat later, 'that the Revolution—as a Russian movement—was intended to make the war efficient'.[63] The very fact that Russia might be the means of opening up the question of peace without complete victory provoked consternation. 'It is difficult to imagine with what keen apprehension and often unconcealed irritation diplomatists in 1917 received our formula of a "democratic peace",' wrote Kerensky.[64] 'If only we can keep them in line until the autumn perhaps some day they will be grateful to us at home,' wrote the British ambassador of his role in keeping up pressure on the Provisional government. A British Labour and French Socialist delegation was even sent to keep up pressure. There has been much discussion of German subsidies to the Bolsheviks but there was another large, but less talked about, Allied flow of cash into the funds of defencist groups and parties.[65] Behind Allied demands that Russia should continue to play a leading role were both its role in the wider imperialist deals that were part of the war effort and the particular military logic of the time. The infamous June offensive, which crumbled after preliminary success and so helped the wider demoralisation of the army, had originally been planned in 1916 as part of a joint Western and Eastern Front attack on Germany. Indeed the Provisional government boasted to the Allies that it had prevented Russian exit from the war in spring 1917 and that 'the greatest number of German divisions throughout the war was concentrated on the Russian front during the summer of 1917'.[66] Even as late as September 1917 Allied representatives and ambassadors continued to pressure the Provisional government, prepared to have in the background the threat that credits and loans might be affected if Russia withdrew.

Under pressure from the soviet the Provisional government was forced to make gestures towards a general peace. But it did so with no belief in what it was doing, happy to hide behind the Allies who, as Wade says, destroyed any peace possibilities with little resistance from their own socialists.[67] There were those at the top who did speculate that Russia had to be pulled out of the war but what is interesting is how little hearing they got.[68] Even Kerensky, who could appear quite radical criticising the war as a struggle for world mastery, grew more committed rather than less over time. After the July crisis his biographer notes that 'never again did he call for a peace without annexations or contributions'.[69] In September and October, when 'the plight of the troops went from unbearable to the unimaginable', General Verkhovsky, the minister of war called not for a separate peace but a stronger initiative for a general peace and he was simply sent on sick leave, so wild did those at top still consider this idea.[70]

The battle for landed property

Maintaining Russia as a great imperial power would mean nothing if the ruling class could not retain control of its economic power and in 1917 this meant that the decisive battles were over land and industry. Yet in respect of land, the polarisation was already huge in the spring of 1917. Shingarev, the first Provisional government minister of agriculture, said in May that he was receiving 100 telegrams a day about the arbitrary rule of peasant committees and the threat to private land ownership. In that month too Read notes:

> The first major congress representing the popular movement was the national Congress of Soviets of Peasants' Deputies that met in Petrograd in early May. It had 1,115 delegates. Fourteen were Bolsheviks. Almost half were SRs. Its main action was to pass overwhelmingly a resolution on land that declared, 'The right of private property in land is abolished forever... Hired labour is not permitted'.[71]

Peasant attitudes are sometimes portrayed as irrational but the resentment of landlordism reflected in motions like this had grown up over the generations and was socialised into each new generation and reinforced by the poverty and oppression of everyday life that so many rural inhabitants experienced. Kirnosov, a peasant deputy in the first Duma, dismissed a landlord defence of property rights with the cutting comment that peasants well understood what was at stake: 'We know your idea of property; my uncle [a serf] was exchanged for a greyhound.' Observers in 1917 found the same bitterness when peasants were told to wait for the land: 'My grandfather, my father and I paid so many taxes for our five dessyatins [13 acres] here, that the land could be quite covered with the money that we gave for it. My father and I were made to pay 36 roubles every year, and to get that money in the old days cost us plenty of sweat and blood'.[72]

Nothing less than the confiscation of the landlords' land would satisfy the aspirations of the peasantry but this encountered several difficulties. An immediate one was that land redistribution might disrupt the war effort, but behind this were two other problems. One was that the landlords could hardly be expected to be enthusiastic (and they were not simply the aristocracy as the land sales had been going on apace since 1861).[73] The second was that much of the financial system rested on loans that were secured on land so that any confiscation threatened the wider stability of the economy. The Provisional government (and indeed in the past the Cadets) argued that it had nothing in principle against land redistribution provided it was supported by the Constituent Assembly and went through proper channels. However, a different agenda was clearly in place at the top of Russian society.[74] As critics on the left pointed out, the talk of the dangers of land confiscation, turmoil and disturbances in the villages, and financial instability all suggested that what was at stake was not respect for the Constituent Assembly but resistance to the confiscation of land itself. 'This argument applies in general to the confiscation of land even if it were undertaken by the Constituent Assembly. It is advanced therefore by supporters of landowners and large scale capital who do not want any real change in the countryside, who want to consolidate the influence of the landowners and money lenders'.[75]

It is not surprising then to find Russia's landowners organising increasingly vigorously throughout 1917 to oppose the revolution. The biggest landowners began to organise a pressure group. In 1905 the All-Russian Union of Landowners had been formed but this had withered with the decline of peasant unrest after 1907. Then in late 1916 there were attempts to create a new union, bringing together those with more than 50 dessyatins, to assist in the war effort. After the February Revolution this union became the organising force for the defence of landowners' interests, joining with the Cadets to try to resist change in the countryside. District and province meetings were held and in May 1917 some 300 delegates from 31 provinces came together in Moscow for the Constituent Congress of the All-Russian Union of Landowners and Farmers. 'Your property, your labours and your expenditures are in danger,' wrote the secretary of the newly formed Council of the Congress.[76] Policies were clarified, not least by the effective alliance with the Cadets, to fight against any attempt to confiscate land worked by those owners who were developing their holdings. On 25 May a draft law was issued banning land sales pending the Constituent Assembly. The union attacked this as a violation of the rights of property, working with the banks who saw the draft law as a threat to the stability of financial markets which was underpinned by existing and potential land sales. As a result, to the dismay of many peasants, the law was effectively dropped. Then in the first week of July the union held its All-Russian Congress with 400 delegates, resolving that if landowners were to 'fulfil their duty to the motherland and to hand over the harvest to it, then [the government] should categorically forbid land committees to take away land, equipment and livestock and to deprive them of labour'. When Chernov became minister of agriculture the union kept up a constant war of attrition against him.[77] Pressure from the landowners was also increased when the Assembly of Notables met in early August and this fed into the Kornilov revolt at the end of the month. The landowners' union also intensified the attempt to use the courts to hold back the peasantry.

This brought direct conflict with the peasantry. 'One can only be struck by the solidarity of [their] community,' writes Read. The scale of peasant violence is a much debated issue but Read suggests that it may have been kept down due to the belief that finally the Constituent Assembly would deliver the land.[78] But one reflection of the success of the landowners can be seen in military actions the Provisional government was persuaded to take against the peasantry. Between May and June there were only 11, whereas in July and August 39 took place and in September and October there were 105 military actions along with arrests of up to 2,000 land committee members responsible, as the government and local authorities saw it, for going too far. Many of these were small but the rising scale was not lost on observers. Moreover in September they culminated in a major confrontation in Tambov where peasant hostility was such that the local landowners, local government and the national government were forced to compromise and back down, prefiguring the surge of peasant hostility and land redistribution that would follow the October Revolution.

The frontier of control in industry

But if the survival of bourgeois Russia meant the defence of land ownership then it depended even more on the control of industry. If the revolution was no more than a bourgeois revolution what rights and long term future did the factory committees and soviets have? Already in May Miliukov attacked radicalism, asking, 'What reason is there for continuing the revolution?' Skobelev, the Menshevik minister of labour, argued similarly at the end of May that 'we find ourselves in the bourgeois stage of revolution. The transfer of enterprises into the hands of the people would not at the present time assist the revolution'.[79]

In fact the attitude of industrialists changed during 1917 as their position worsened. In the early days of the revolution the initiative in industrial circles passed to businessmen like A I Konovalov, a cotton entrepreneur and vice-chairman of the Moscow stock exchange, whose firms, said Miliukov, 'were famous for the brilliant way in which they handled the labour question'.[80] With some other businessmen from the Moscow region Konovalov had aspired to more modern 'European' business and labour practices. This led him into conflict with the Tsarist government and industrialists in the Petrograd area who, he believed, too much favoured workplace and government repression of labour rather than the enlightened self interest of more positive workplace policies. After February he and like minded businessmen had a decisive sway. Pavel Riabushinskii could even describe the first Provisional government as 'our regime'.[81] In the so called 'honeymoon period' of March and early April it looked possible to reconstruct labour relations by recognising unions, conceding the eight hour day and a large wage increase to take account of inflation, and establishing conciliation boards to deal with conflicts. Debates still existed over the wisdom of this programme and some industrialists were unhappy that the government should play a role in what they considered 'their' field, but there can be no doubt that there was considerable movement.

But the growing class contradictions of 1917 soon undercut this strategy and employers who, like workers, were organising apace in various associations soon began to swing in a more hostile direction. In opposition to the growing demands from below Konovalov, in Miliukov's words, 'preferred to resign on 18 May without even finding a replacement for himself. In vain he was urged to remain at his post... This was the first answer from the "bourgeois" members of the [first] coalition to the unfeasible part of the coalition's programme.' By the summer of 1917 'pessimism, suspicion and intransigence had come to dominate the entrepreneurs' dealings with the Provisional government, with their socialist partners in the cabinet and above all with the workers'.[82]

This was because the employers perceived a threat to stability, their profits and the very existence of their firms. During 1917 the economic crisis continued to develop.[83] Inflation soared as the Provisional government struggled to finance the war but found it difficult to raise taxes or get its loans taken up. Industrial production continued to be squeezed by the war. This helped to perpetuate a vicious circle where peasants were reluctant to sell grain to the towns which were producing little they wanted to buy. Attempts to fix prices and even early examples of grain requisitioning failed to alleviate the difficulties. The strain on transport grew too, further disrupting the distribution of food, raw materials and finished goods. In June 1917 a Conference on Defence Supplies was told that 'the state of industry is catastrophic'. By August the Ministry of Supplies could say that the 'country is faced with the grim spectre of famine'.[84]

The situation was made worse by the increasing expectations of workers and the fact that the indecisiveness of local and national government meant that industrialists could no longer confidently trust it as 'theirs'. This was reinforced by the pattern of strikes which went down immediately after February but rose from April to the July crisis, declining in July but rising prior to the Kornilov coup, falling in early September as the coup was defeated and then rising again in late September to early October 1917.[85]

Much has been made by some social historians of the fact that when the workplace committees spoke of workers' 'kontrol' the Russian term has a weaker meaning than 'control' in English, suggesting more the idea of supervision. But if the early demands of the factory committees for 'kontrol' were less radical than is sometimes imagined then the growing crisis forced a redefinition. As Smith puts it, 'The policy of workers' control of production was first and foremost an attempt by factory committees to stem the tide of industrial chaos'.[86] But to stem the tide the conception of 'kontrol' had to move closer and closer to that of 'control' in the English sense.[87] From the employers' point of view this meant that their prerogatives were increasingly challenged as the frontier of control was pushed outwards by the factory committees and workers were radicalised by the crisis. In reply employers tried to draw the line, 'We are now prepared to rebuff the attack on private property,' said one. 'You must defend yourselves by establishing an organisation that will establish unity.' As Galili puts it, 'In the post-July period the Moscow industrialists, both those led by Riabushinskii in the All-Russian Commercial-Industrial Union and those headed by Guzhon in the Moscow Society of Factory and Mill Owners, made confrontation their declared aim'.[88]

This switch in position by the most 'progressive group' is easily understandable in terms of not only their disappointment with the results of February but also the specific way in which the economic crisis affected them. The core of the early difficulties was in the textile industry of the central industrial region, especially the provinces of Moscow, Vladimir, Riazan, Kaluga and Kostroma. Here shortages of fuel and raw materials immensely complicated the problems of industrialists and caused plants to close. In the March-July period 133 plants shut in these provinces with an average of 530 workers each, making up 68 percent of recorded jobs lost. Overall 8 percent of cotton plants closed with 12 percent of the industry workforce and 30 percent of the silk workforce lost their employment. It was in August-September that the crisis hit the metal working industry harder. Until then only 91 of the plants that had closed had been in this sector with an average size of 120 workers. Now around a third of the 231 plants closing were in metal working with an average of over 300 workers each, making up some 55 percent of the incompletely reported workforce losses. Moreover the spiral was continuing downwards throughout 1917. In the Donets only 80 million poods of coal were mined in October when 52 million poods were needed for the railways alone. Industrial supplies were to be only one third of what was needed.[89]

As we shall see this led sections of the industrialists straight into the arms of Kornilov. Even after his coup failed the pressure remained to fight to push back the frontier of control. This accounts for the way in September that, to the consternation of those on the left who believed that some comprise with capital remained possible, even moderate groups of workers suddenly found themselves under pressure from the employers.[90]

Russia—one and indivisible

As we have seen, the concept of Russia 'one and indivisible' was a unifying force in the ruling class before 1914. Some liberals might have thought in terms of a 'United States of Russia' or looked admiringly at the supposed integration of the British Empire as alternatives to Tsarist oppression but they shared a concern to maintain the integrity of the Russian state. This was challenged in 1917 by left-leaning nationalist movements but, rather than make generous concessions, liberals tried to hold on to a larger Russia. The Cadet leadership was even prepared to do this though it antagonised its own members in areas like the Ukraine.

The one concession that was quickly made was the acceptance of independence for Poland. However, this was less radical than it appeared since Poland was under enemy occupation and if Germany was defeated and a new Polish state was created it would have to include parts of what were Germany and Austria. This could be to Russia's advantage, as could the fact that Poland would be a large buffer state in central Europe. Beyond this there was resistance to change even amongst those who ostensibly supported claims for national self determination. Kerensky told the First Congress of Soviets, 'Today I say only one thing—I recognise the rights of the Ukraine and Finland, but cannot agree to their separation until the Constituent Assembly of the Russian people has sanctioned it '.[91] This argument was especially provocative in Finland where, when Nicholas abdicated as emperor of Russia he also abdicated as Grand Duke of Finland (a title he held separately). Power should therefore have reverted to the Finnish assembly. Moreover this assembly had, for the time, relatively impeccable democratic credentials, having been elected by universal suffrage. In addition deputies from Finland were not to be elected to the Constituent Assembly making nonsense of the argument for waiting for 'self determination'.

Nevertheless when the Finnish Sejm voted for autonomy in July 1917 the Provisional government dissolved it. It did not take much to see another agenda at work here. Not the least of the problems was that granting Finnish independence might encourage other national groups to demand the same rights to self determination especially those in the Ukraine. Then it was argued that 'Russia's interests' in the war had to have priority and Finland, where pro-German elements were powerful, might become a base for the enemy close to Petrograd. This was overlaid by the idea that fine words from the Provisional government should be taken at face value and could somehow dissipate the suspicion of Russian motives inculcated by Tsarist oppression, an idea which to the oppressed nationalities looked like great Russian chauvinism dressed up in democratic clothes.

The issue of the Ukraine was even more sensitive because it was so much more central to the idea of 'Russia'. Moreover in the Constituent Assembly elections in the Ukraine over 70 percent voted for nationalist parties. This radicalisation reflected complex motives, and the conflict between the idea of 'Russian', 'Ukrainian' and other local identities versus the possibility of more internationalist ideas has recently received much attention. But while Russia's new rulers were happy to implement some form of autonomy, what mattered above all in Moscow and Petrograd in 1917 was keeping the Ukraine in Russia. It was the Ukrainian issue that broke the first coalition of the Provisional government. On 10 June the Ukrainian Rada proclaimed the autonomy of the Ukraine and called for a national assembly. Members of the Provisional government agreed to recognise the Rada if nationalists reduced their demands until the Constituent Assembly met. But this was too much for the Cadets who saw separatism as German inspired and 'yet another link in the German plan to break Russia up'. For Miliukov it represented 'the chopping up of Russia under the slogan of self determination'. It was, as he says in his memoirs, the 'betrayal of Russia's interests'. While he recognised the need to make some gesture towards autonomy his attitude is reflected in his language: both the Finns and Ukrainians were 'striving to take advantage of Russia's troubles' but whereas the Finns were 'cautious and subtle' the Ukrainian nationalists were 'fanatics'.[92] As the Cadets left the Provisional government, Kerensky denounced them. 'On the front, thousands are giving up their lives—and you here, you desert your posts and smash the govern-ment.' But Miliukov and the Cadet leaders well understood both their support for the idea of 'Russia' and the politics of July. Once the insurgency of the workers in the capital in early July was defeated they were able to exercise a controlling influence over the new second coalition government whose Cadet ministers were 'virtually hand-picked by Miliukov'.[93]

This attempt to hold the line against the claims of national self determination continued into the autumn. Even on the eve of October the minister of foreign affairs, Tereshchenko, who reputedly could not even pronounce the word Ukraine, was still denouncing the idea of independence for even the Baltic states as inconsistent with the position of Russia as a great power.

The Kornilov coup

All of these conflicts pointed to a fundamental choice in the summer of 1917 which Miliukov formulated as 'Lenin or Kornilov'—the general who attempted a coup. In reality the 'coup' that resulted was a disaster, a confused attempt to take power which collapsed without shots being fired in anger. But in the process it destroyed any remaining credit that the government, army high command and the political class had with the mass of the urban population. The hostile reaction to it caused a renewed national surge to the left whose main beneficiary was the Bolshevik Party. Controversy continues to rage over whether it was a coup at all and how serious a threat it presented. George Katkov denounces the idea that a coup was ever intended as a 'lunatic theory', a product of Kerensky's fevered imagination.[94]

Such dismissals fail to engage with the tensions and uncertainties that afflict both left and right alike in revolutionary situations. No less than a revolutionary seizure of power, a coup from the right is a leap in the dark that cannot be meticulously planned. If it works then everything that happened was intended and a tribute to the foresight of the plotters. If it fails then the defence becomes it was never really intended, the coup organisers had misunderstood what was meant and so on. All of this is clearly apparent in the story of the Kornilov coup. Had it worked key sections of the Russian political class were ready to line up behind it as its 'loyal supporters'. But when it failed they cashed in their insurance policies in an attempt to get themselves off the hook.

The attempted coup was the result of the coming together of two logics. The first was the concern of sections of the officer class in the army to impose order on the troops and to have a government that would support the military.[95] General Kornilov was appointed commander in chief of the Russian armies on 18 July to replace Brusilov who had lost the support of all sides. On the South Western Front Kornilov had adopted 'an uncompromising stand towards the military committees' in the army. By late June when the offensive of the Eighth Army brought some success he was convinced that 'a firm statement from the commander coupled with determined action was necessary to arrest the army's disintegration'. On the 7-8 July, now commander in chief on the South Western Front, to stop the retreat, he:

> ...at once demanded that the commanding officers take decisive measures against traitors and renegades, notifying them that I was assuming full responsibility for such action. I ordered that deserters and looters be shot, and that the bodies of those executed be displayed prominently at the roadsides, with appropriate inscriptions attached to them.[96]

Meetings at the front were banned and shock battalions of officer cadets were formed 'to combat desertion, marauding and violence'. His elevation to commander in chief therefore was a clear political statement by the Provisional government, and Kornilov was just as anxious that they should understand his position. He immediately tried to impose three conditions. Rather than reject them the Provisional government fudged and conceded that he should be responsible to his conscience and the nation (ie not the government); that there should be no interference with his operational orders or appointments; and that measures applied at the front, including the death penalty, should also be applied to the army in the rear.[97] He then moved to try to insist on a more total militarisation of the whole war effort telling a conference at General Headquarters on 30 July, in words he recalled a month later, 'We must have three armies: one fighting in the trenches, another workers' army in the rear and another consisting of railwaymen.' The implementation of this was a task for the Provisional government but 'such armies should be governed by the same iron discipline as now at present enforced in the armies at the front'.[98]

The second logic arose from the wider class struggle and the coming together of sections of the ruling class around a more determined defence of capitalism. It was defeat of the partial uprising of the July Days in Petrograd that marked the change in climate. L'vov, though forced out of office in favour of Kerensky as prime minister, saw this clearly: 'It is my firm conviction that our deep breach on the Lenin front has incomparably more importance for Russia than the breach made by the Germans on the South Western Front'.[99] This was reflected in the character of the new second coalition of the Provisional government. In the words of Miliukov, 'With a slight preponderance of socialists, the actual preponderance in the cabinet unquestionably belonged to the convinced partisans of bourgeois democracy.' To which Trotsky later famously added his comment that 'it would be more accurate to say bourgeois property'.[100]

A succession of measures quickly followed as the atmosphere at the top of society grew more hostile to the revolution from below in all its forms. On 8 July the military regulations were tightened; the death penalty reintroduced on 12 July and a major meeting of the government and the generals took place on 16 July. In the countryside a public order decree of 6 July made it an offence to incite attacks on private property, on 8 July the government again insisted that land seizures were not allowable. By mid-July Chernov, the new and ostensibly more left wing minister of agriculture, was trying to define and limit the powers of land committees. In areas at the front under the control of the army, peasant demonstrations were banned. In industry too the turn was clear and by mid-August Skobolev, the Menshevik minister of labour, was trying, under pressure, to reduce the power the factory committees.

On 3 August at the Trade Industrialists Conference in Moscow Riabushinbski had insisted that 'we ought to say...that the present revolution is a bourgeois revolution, that the bourgeois order which exists at present is inevitable, and since it is inevitable, one must draw the logical conclusion and insist that those who rule the state think in a bourgeois manner and act in a bourgeois manner...' This signal was understood not only by the left. For *Rech*, the Cadet paper, this was 'an occasion where the bourgeoisie finally strikes back...'[101] At the Moscow State Conference (between 12-15 August) Kornilov spoke but, left it to General Denikin to represent what was been called 'the authentic voice of the Russian generals', and the polarisation became even clearer. Even the sceptical Katkov is forced to admit that:

> One thing that was crystal clear to all present was that a gathering like this could never beget a new parliament, or indeed any other body representative of the whole nation, on which the government could rely. Not even the most innocently worded resolution could now be put to the vote without revealing the chasm that had opened up in Russian society.[102]

But the bourgeoisie was actually split on how to move forward. Already in the spring V S Zavoiko, a man with wide business links which stretched from Petrograd to the Baku oil industry, had helped to link together leading Petrograd industrialists and bankers as well as other interested parties like the publisher B A Suvorin. Zavoiko also helped to reinforce connections for this group with sections of the army. Related to them was the industrialist A I Putilov who established the Society for the Economic Rehabilitation of Russia. Their initial aim had been to produce conservative propaganda to limit the revolution and to support right wing candidates for the Constituent Assembly. But as the revolution developed perceptions began to change. The All-Russian Congress of Trade and Industry at the start of August, followed by the State Conference, both held in Moscow, allowed contacts to be developed. The exact story of the plotting and meetings remains disputed but it is clear that the liberal Moscow based businessmen, while growing increasingly hostile to the revolution, still wished to bide their time. This was the direction of Riabushinskii's infamous speech at the Trade Congress from which the phrase 'bony hand of hunger' is often quoted out of context. What he actually said was:

> *Therefore, gentlemen, we have to wait—this catastrophe, this financial-economic failure, will be inevitable for Russia, if we are not already facing catastrophe, and when it becomes obvious to everybody only then will they feel that they have been taking the wrong road... We feel that this is inevitable. But unfortunately it is necessary for the bony hand of hunger and poverty to grab the false friends of the people by the throat, the members of the committees and soviets, in order that they should understand this.*[103]

However, the Petrograd group was much more active. Deriving from those sections of capital which had developed the closest links with Tsarism (including through military production) they more naturally looked to the army for support after February and now saw in Kornilov a way forward. They were supported in this by wider sections of the upper classes fearing for their future and seeing him as a potential saviour. Individuals wrote to him urging action. 'Letters', he said, 'came flooding in from all over the country describing acts of violence perpetrated against landowners and a complete breakdown in every sector of national life'.[104] The Cadet party began to debate what position it should take. Throughout July and August it had moved further to the right. Although the Cadets were a secular party it was even beginning to make its peace with the Orthodox Church whose leadership were anxious about their future role in Russia. Tyrkova, on the right of the party, told the Cadet leadership on 20 August that the Cadets 'must support a dictator even more than Kerensky; there is no other way, only through blood.' Miliukov, said his fellow Cadet Maklakov, treated the possibility of a coup as 'an accomplished fact' and therefore the only issue was 'to find the right attitude to take towards it'. To this end Miliukov was happy to allow Kornilov to believe that he had his active support whereas he was in fact trying to have a foot in both camps in case Kornilov failed. According to General Denikin, Maklakov told him at the time, 'Tell General Kornilov that we are all of us inciting him to act, Miliukov especially. In fact nobody is going to support General Kornilov—they are all going to watch from the sidelines'.[105]

What was happening was clearly sensed by sections of the popular movement. As Read puts it:

> From the ordinary soldiers' and sailors' point of view... the new conjuncture was clear. The authorities were on the offensive in the army and navy just as they were in the factories and villages. The period from July to August saw the most concerted effort of the whole revolutionary period to slow down and even control the popular movement.[106]

Tension rose throughout August. On 20 August Riga fell to the Germans and then news arrived that a major munitions supply dump in Kazan had exploded with the loss of a million shells and 12,000 machine guns. The officer class was further antagonised by the news that troops had murdered General Hirschfeld and a prominent political commissar, Linde. What happened next is still surrounded in confusion. Essentially, it appears that at some stage the pretext of a Bolshevik uprising in Petrograd (some officers even had to be dissuaded from creating a riot to simulate this) would be used as the justification for sending troops into the capital. At the last moment Kerensky, having either by his complicity or weakness done nothing to stop the build up to decisive action by Kornilov, saw a chance to denounce him and remove his challenge and, he hoped, restore his declining credibility with the popular base of the revolution. By turning on Kornilov at the key moment he may have unwittingly saved the revolution but his desperate gamble failed not least because no fighting took place to back up his own account of his stand against the general. Instead General Alekseev successfully mediated with Kornilov as his troops faded away under the impact of the denunciation of Kornilov's actions and the propaganda of the rapidly mobilised workforce of Petrograd. Without the glory of a whiff of 'grapeshot' to bolster him Kerensky suddenly found his own actions exposed to the glare of publicity and humiliation. He had temporarily removed a challenge from the army but was himself now in an even weaker position in terms of public support.

Political choices post-Kornilov

A revolutionary crisis, it has been said, is a moment of truth when the divisions in a society are exposed and a political choice stands starkly before the contesting classes. We have already argued that far from the policy of the Provisional government being a series of 'mistakes', what happened between February and August reflected the way in which the interests of the ruling class conflicted with those of the popular movement without 'bourgeois democracy' offering the possibility of a solution. The Kornilov coup was a response on the part of sections of the ruling class to this dilemma. When it failed, the initiative, at least for the moment, passed to the left but the underlying problems that divided society remained unresolved. Indeed the pressure grew worse in September and October making the political response of the parties concerned the supreme question.

In our understanding of this, however, we encounter something of a paradox. In one sense we are better informed of the dynamics of the popular movement in the final revolutionary crisis than ever before. This is a result of the mass of fine work produced in the West in the last two decades. But much of this work has come from social historians who have been so concerned with the popular movement that they have dangerously devalued the political choices made in late 1917. This has had a number of unfortunate consequences. Two are crucial here. The first is the devaluation of what we can call 'the party political choice'—the understanding of the way in which the political, policy and organisational strengths and weaknesses of parties were ruthlessly tested in the crisis. The second devaluation can be seen in the 'sociologism' of the analysis of the popular movement (and especially the factory workers) where the swing to support the Bolsheviks is almost presented as a gut response to crisis rather than an expression of a conscious political choice between competing political alternatives.

This failure to build a properly political dimension into the understanding of the crisis has left the analysis of many of these 'social historians' of the revolution vulnerable. Faced with the resurgence of a more conservative approach to the revolution many have beaten a hasty retreat rather than refine their work. The result is what we can call a 'Menshevik' approach to the 'moment of truth' in October. On the left the term Menshevik has so often been used as a term of abuse that we hesitate to use it here lest it be misunderstood as simple pejorative labelling. But the term is the correct one in two senses. Firstly some historians, most notably Vladimir Brovkin, openly identify with the Menshevik case in developing a critique of the Bolshevik seizure of power. Secondly, the wider discussion echoes the basic Menshevik claim that the Bolsheviks took advantage of a temporarily favourable conjunction to take power in such a way that they could not hope to maintain their popular base for more than a short time. They would therefore be forced to rule over it, rather than with it. In some cases this weakness in the understanding of the political in the autumn of 1917 is then reinforced by another historiographical retreat in the form of a lurch towards postmodernism. If political choices are constructed at the level of language and 'discourse' then the clarity of the moment of truth at the top is diminished—it is not so much a creation of objective circumstances as the 'ideological prism' through which the situation is understood. Equally the swing to the left at the bottom becomes even less an expression of a politicised consciousness and more a response constructed from distorted symbolism and a language of conflict and violence.[107]

In order therefore to conclude our discussion of why 'bourgeois democracy' failed in 1917 we must first address the issue of the 'party political choice' in the autumn before dealing more briefly with the nature of the choices made in the popular movement.

The crisis intensifies

In the wake of the Kornilov coup the second Provisional government coalition fell apart as Cadet ministers were discredited and resigned. Kerensky desperately tried to form a 'third coalition' but the question was now whether the bourgeoisie and the Cadets had not so harmed themselves as to be completely untrustworthy partners. This question was made more pointed still by the fact that although the balance of power had swung to the left nothing else had changed—there was still conflict over democracy, the war, land, the factories and the empire—all splitting Russia apart. Kerensky therefore formed a five man 'directory' on 1 September to run the government while a new coalition was put together, which took until 25 September.[108]

The weeks of the directory and then the final month of the third coalition saw the further crumbling of authority of the government which vasillated erratically as it clung to power. Ignoring the argument that no fundamental changes could be made without the Constituent Assembly, Kerensky tried to improve his standing by declaring Russia a republic on 5 September. This outraged the Cadets who argued that he had no authority for the move. The Senate—which had survived from the pre-February days, declared against the move until, on 6 October, Kerensky dissolved it and the old state Duma (which had continued to have meetings since February although without a formal role).[109] On the other hand, the government kept up pressure on the peasants and outraged many on the left by declaring martial law in Tashkent. As September progressed into October Kerensky began to look towards a confrontation believing that he could smash a Bolshevik uprising. He told Nabokov, 'I would be prepared to offer prayers to produce this uprising... I have greater forces than necessary. They will be utterly crushed'.[110]

To try to get some base for the government the executives of the urban and rural Congresses of Soviets, in conjunction with Kerensky, called an All-Russian Democratic Conference from 14-22 September. The 1,582 delegates (including 532 SRs, 172 Mensheviks, 136 Bolsheviks and 55 Trudoviks) were immediately paralysed by the question of whether there could be a coalition with the bourgeoisie in general and the Cadets in particular.[111] Before the conference closed it elected the so called Pre- Parliament or Provisional Council of the Republic which eventually met on 7 October. Having helped to call these bodies into existence Kerensky refused to submit the Provisional government to them on the grounds that it was the supreme repository of state power until the Constituent Assembly met and therefore responsible to itself. The Cadets even objected to the title since Russia had not been legally made a republic in their eyes. The same polarisation again emerged. As Galili puts it, 'Census Russia again seemed bent on a strategy of confrontation'.[112] The Bolsheviks therefore boycotted the Pre-Parliament, followed by the Petrograd Soviet. They also brought considerable pressure on the reluctant Executive of the Soviets to call the Second All-Russian Congress of Soviets. Despite their fears of the composition of such a Second Congress the existing Soviet Executive was forced to agree and on 23 September called the Second Congress for late October.

The confrontation evident at the political level continued also in the economy. Employers were now finding it hard to survive and it is difficult to distinguish between workers being dismissed because of difficulties in maintaining production and those dismissed because employers were getting out while they could. The Provisional government and the Soviet leadership again equivocated in their response. In Petrograd, for example, 'the *Putilovtsy* faced the October Revolution with one third of their factory facing redundancy thrust upon them by their own supposed representatives in the Soviet and the Provisional government'. At the Fourth Congress of Factory Committees Skrypnik said 'We are no longer standing in the ante-chamber of economic collapse; we have entered the zone of collapse itself'.[113]

Petrograd, located in the far north of Russia and dependent on supplies from the centre and the south, felt the crisis in an extreme way. Food was growing scarce. In the first days of October only 30 grain wagons arrived instead of the 500 needed to supply the city. 'In Petrograd', said a writer in *Rabochii Put'* in mid-October, 'there is no bread, meat, milk—least of all for the poor classes, for the workers and employees; though there is always sufficient quantity for the well-to-do strata of the population. All these goods are always available to the capitalists.' Rationing became more widespread; when supplies diminished, rations were cut and even these then proved hard to deliver to the mass of the population.

The government's response continued to falter and in trying to solve one problem it seemed to accentuate another. Trying to raise the price of grain, said a motion pushed through the Petrograd City Duma:

> ...is only advantageous to the owners of large grain stores.....; the greatest weight falls with scandalous unfairness on the urban poor and the needy strata of the peasantry. And therefore the City Duma, forced to raise a tax on bread [by putting up prices], disclaims all responsibility for this, placing it wholly on the policy of the Provisional government.[114]

In the popular movement it seemed that only the attempt to organise things from below was holding the line against chaos. 'The organisation of workers' control is a manifestation of the same healthy activity in the sphere of industrial production as are party organisations in the sphere of politics, trade unions in employment, co-operatives in the domain of consumption and literary clubs in the sphere of culture,' said the First All-Russian Congress of Factory Committees, just prior to the revolution in October.

> The working class has much more interest in the proper and uninterrupted operation of the factories...than the capitalist class. Workers' control is a better security in this respect for the interests of modern society, of the whole people, than the arbitrary will of the owners, who are guided only by their selfish desire for material profits or political privileges. Therefore workers' control is demanded by the proletariat not only in their own interest, but in the interests of the whole country, and should be supported by the revolutionary peasantry as well as the revolutionary army.[115]

At the political level this meant that a new government was needed that would end the compromises of the Provisional government in all its forms. As Leonard Schapiro put it, 'Any objective and honest student of 1917 in Russia cannot fail to observe the fact that by September or October the majority of the articulate portions of the Russian population had rejected the leadership of the middle class parties, and stood for a soviet government composed of a coalition of all socialist parties represented in the soviets throughout the country'.[116] The question was now how would the left respond?

The Bolshevik response

It is commonplace to accuse the Bolsheviks of being opportunist in October 1917. But this charge fits ill with the evidence of intense debate between 1914 and 1917 on the nature of the crisis and its resolution within the party. If we are able to use hindsight to reformulate the argument that emerged with more sharpness, this does not alter the fact that the shift in ideas was far more impressive than that in any other group, left or right. The explanation for this, though hostile historians are loathe to admit it, is that the Bolshevik Party was both theoretically and politically more flexible than the rest of the left and had to travel less far in terms of its politics in 1917. Thus despite the debates within the Bolshevik Party the effect of the radicalisation in 1917 was to remake the party and drive it towards revolution, a quite different impact from that which it had on the rest of the left.

The starting point for Lenin, Trotsky, Bukharin and others was that they were living in a new and increasingly integrated world of imperialism in which the capacity for autonomous development was limited by the growing power of advanced capitalist states. These were prepared to supplement economic competition with military competition and, if necessary, war. This created two tendencies which worked to the advantage of socialism. One was a tendency to ever greater state control, what Bukharin called state capitalism, in which the ever growing units of private capital intermeshed with units of state capital and so made democratic socialist control a more realistic possibility. The second was the way the ever growing integration made it possible for workers in a state like Russia to be able to inaugurate what was a process of more general revolution—part of the basis of what Trotsky called permanent revolution. War accentuated these tendencies further. But the daily bloodshed on the Western and Eastern fronts as well as in the 'sideshows' also exemplified that the choice could be one between 'socialism and barbarism'. Even if the war were brought quickly to a close, internal and external conflicts no less barbaric would emerge.

Within Russia the specific crisis had created the most militant working class in the world alongside a peasantry and army whose revolt was also growing by the day. It had also created democratic structures of committees and soviets the like of which the world had not seen before. Within these the Bolsheviks had been pushed to the fore:

*We are on the threshold of a world proletarian revolution. And since of all the proletarian internationalists in all countries only we Russian Bolsheviks enjoy a measure of freedom—we have a legal party and a score or so of papers, we have the Soviets of Workers' and Soldiers' Deputies of both capitals on our side, and we have the support of the **majority** of the people in a time of revolution—to us the saying, 'To whom much has been* *given, of him much shall be required,' in all justice can and must be applied.*

Not to take this chance risked enormous dangers. The unprecedented scale and speed with which the crisis was still developing meant that either the revolution would succeed or the Tsarist empire would collapse in on itself or be held together by a second Kornilov revolt which would not only destroy the Bolsheviks but carry away the other parties of soviet democracy and its very institutions with them. 'History will not forgive us if we do not assume power now'; 'It is impossible to stand still in history in general, and in wartime in particular. We must either advance or retreat,' Lenin kept insisting:

> *The complete disruption of Russia's economic life has now reached a point where catastrophe is unavoidable, a catastrophe of such appalling dimensions that a number of essential industries will be brought to a standstill, the farmer will be prevented from conducting farming on the necessary scale, and the railway traffic will be interrupted with a consequent stoppage of grain deliveries to the industrial population and the cities involving millions of people. What is more, the breakdown has already started, and has affected various industries.*[117]

These positions were not arrived at automatically. They involved debates that were if anything sharper than those in other left parties. In April the Bolshevik Party was divided, again in July, again in September-October over the issue of taking power and then again and again after October. These debates continued into the 1920s until they were finally crushed by emerging Stalinism. Far from Lenin dominating a monolith as both Stalinist and right wing historical writing in the West suggests, the party in 1917 was suffused with debate. Indeed we can stand the normal argument on its head and say that it was just because the party had both a focus on the popular movement and a vigorous tradition of sharp and serious debates that it was able to generate the clear positions that allowed it to function as well as it did. The contrast with its competitors could not be clearer.

The political failure of the SRs and the Mensheviks

It is possible to have an argument with the Bolshevik analysis but what is striking is the failure of both SR and Menshevik theorists to advance a counter-argument of any depth. Instead they remained stuck in an argument that had not advanced beyond the pre-war days. Both the main groups of SRs and the Mensheviks still operated with the more or less coherent idea that the revolution had to be a bourgeois one.[118] Yet by now they were also arguing that it was no longer possible to work with the bourgeoisie which had opposed the revolution and was looking to civil war. Equally, however, they rejected the idea of a socialist coalition which would include the Bolsheviks since this would alienate the bourgeoisie and risk throwing such a coalition government into the hands of the 'extremists'. Instead they tried to occupy the middle ground supporting a coalition with the right socialists (with or without Kerensky). This produced a position which was theoretically and politically unworkable and this was clear both to the right and the left, and often to the SR and Menshevik leaderships themselves. One interpretation of this is that the Menshevik and SR leaders were afraid of taking power themselves. Lande later wrote that 'lacking confidence in their own ability to govern, they found the theory of the bourgeois character of the Russian Revolution a reassuring excuse'.[119] But this is too easy. Harding is much nearer the mark when he argues that the problem was not courage but politics and though his comment applies specifically to the Mensheviks it can be extended to the centre of the Socialist Revolutionaries:

None of the prominent theorists of Menshevism attempted to keep pace with, or offer substantial criticism of, the theoretical premises which Bukharin and Lenin elaborated in the period 1914 to 1917. The Mensheviks remained rooted in the synthesis of 1905 (economic analysis—comparatively low development of Russian capitalism, derivative political practice—the realisation of the democratic revolution). In 1917 they bitterly criticised Lenin's proposals for an advance to socialist practice but made little or no attempt to confront the theoretical basis from which this was derived. It was they who bucked the argument.[120]

It was Lenin who in 1917 'cut the knot', as Fedor Dan put it. The Menshevik theorists Dan, Martov, etc, failing to cut the knot themselves, floundered between the idea of 'bourgeois revolution' and something beyond it; 'Dan did not appeal to the traditional conception in its pristine purity. Too many holes had been punched in it by the Mensheviks' own amendments, adjustments, and explanations of 1905 and 1917'.[121] Unable to disentangle themselves in any coherent way from the idea of a 'bourgeois revolution' they continued to wriggle on the hook they had created for themselves.

From the right the Cadets hammered away at this inconsistency. By now the party had adopted what Rosenberg calls 'a fully fledged civil war mentality' and its leaders were anxious to draw lines.[122] Miliukov insisted that if the left genuinely believed that the revolution was bourgeois and could not go beyond a bourgeois stage then they had to follow the consequences and accept what Sukhanov had argued for after February, namely that they should allow the bourgeoisie 'to stand at the head of that revolution and carry out their bourgeois affairs'. They argued that a bourgeois revolution without the bourgeoisie, over the opposition of the bourgeoisie, on the backs of a socialist coalition, was simply 'unfeasible' and the mess the attempt achieved vindicated this view.[123] In the Council of the Republic Nabokov and other Cadets made the same argument immediately insisting that the key issue was order and the fight against Bolshevism. As Nabokov saw it, 'Our "leftist friends" were incorrigible, and...all our efforts to reach agreement and support for authority in its fight with anarchy and rebellion had almost gone to waste.' Speaking to Dan and the Mensheviks, Nabokov and the Cadets argued that 'your present attitude is again the old ambiguous, uncertain, "in so far as" kind of confidence which is no help whatever to the government and does not facilitate its task'.[124]

From the right of the Socialist Revolutionaries, Kerensky and the group around him made the same challenge to the centre of his party and the Mensheviks:

> *The Bolsheviks, Social Democrats and Socialist Revolutionaries...are for everything that causes anarchy, refuses to defend the country, or is against unity. Their front is one, and the devastation of Russia moves at a gigantic rate. And the other part of the democracy—the one that sits in session at the Alexandrovsky Theatre—its front united, and what does it intend to do? Does it seriously imagine that it is possible to support the Provisional government...and to continue to seek compromises with...those who sow discord and hostility throughout the Republic, who repudiate at bottom what it asserts...*

Postresov, who led the right wing of Menshevism, denounced the refusal of a coalition with the bourgeoisie, saying this 'is worse than Bolshevism. This is absurdity'.[125]

But how could you have a coalition with a bourgeoisie defending its class interests, wishing to see the popular movement suppressed and toying with counter-revolutionary generals? On what terms should support be given to a succession of 'irresponsible' governments which had failed to satisfy the popular agenda? Yet the revolution had to be 'bourgeois democratic'. This produced a series of bizarre theoretical twists. The left had shifted since February from the position of allowing a bourgeois government to carry out bourgeois tasks; to participation of socialists in a bourgeois government to carry out bourgeois tasks; to opposition to a government of the bourgeoisie in favour of a socialist government which would limit itself to bourgeois democratic tasks. To support this it was now argued in the Menshevik Party that the bourgeoisie had failed so the initiative was passing over to a socialist led revolutionary democracy which could carry out the bourgeois revolution with the support of the 'revolutionary' petty bourgeoisie. This bizarre idea owed more to a desperate analogy with the French Revolution than a credible assessment of the situation in Russia in 1917 which, for all its weaknesses, one of the biggest industrial powers in the world.[126]

The problem was that the situation had changed but the analysis had not, so that, as Galili argues, whereas between February and July 1917 Menshevik ideas 'made for several viable alternatives' the period after July 'was one of mounting hopelessness for the Mensheviks'.[127] The theoretical twists were complimented by political ones. By late September both the SR and Menshevik parties were formally supporting a 'democratic coalition', excluding Cadets, only to find that when Kerensky managed to form the third coalition (in negotiation with leading figures in these parties) it included Cadets and Mensheviks and SRs. Chernov, the most prominent centre SR now under pressure from the left, was outraged when the central committee of the party agreed to endorse the coalition. Amongst the Menshevik leadership an agonised debate took place as they too tried to distance themselves from what the Internationalists called their 'non-representatives' in the government while not going so far as to break all connection with it.

As the agonising continued Kerensky kept up the attack from the right in the Council of the Republic:

I believe (Kerensky addressed the Internationalists) that everyone at the present time must decide whether he is on the side of the republic, freedom and democracy, or against these. (Prolonged applause on all benches, with the exception of the Internationalists). And if there are people who believe that the truth is on the other side, then they must manfully take their place in those ranks, and not behave themselves as they do now. (Storm of applause from the right and centre; noise from the left).

'Noise from the left' but no answer since Kerensky's taunts again exposed from one side of the polarisation the indecision that the Bolsheviks exposed from the other. In turn Dan, one of the key leaders of the Mensheviks, argued that the Bolsheviks had 'openly taken advantage of the real dissatisfaction among the broad masses whose needs have not been met' because of the obstruction 'by classes whose representatives are sitting on the right side' but he then returned to the plaintive cry that the government should deliver a solution on peace (while being forced to recognise that the minister of foreign affairs 'did not say a single word about raising the question of peace negotiations at the Allied Conference') and land.

The collapse of SR and Menshevik support

With these political problems and inconsistencies it is not surprising to find that while Bolshevik support grew rapidly, support for the SRs and Mensheviks flooded away in the summer and autumn of 1917. The pattern of urban elections shows the Bolsheviks were a small minority but a growing one in provincial Russia throughout 1917. In the larger urban centres, however, they were a major presence. Nationally everyone recognised that their performance in Petrograd and Moscow was the litmus test. Both cities had two elections to their city dumas in 1917 and although turnout fell sharply in the second elections large numbers still voted. Rosenberg, the Western historian who has studied these elections most closely, suggests that absenteeism was as much caused by frustration with the lack of progress as apolitical apathy.

In Petrograd the second election took place on 20 August. It shows the recovery in Bolshevik strength after July *before* the Kornilov coup had occurred (indeed the likely result may have added to the case for action from the right). Table 2 clearly demonstrates the swing to the Bolsheviks away from, especially, the Mensheviks in Petrograd but also to some extent the Socialist Revolutionaries. Analysing the results the journal of the Union of Towns commented that:

> *The most striking fact of the elections is the colossal strengthening of the Bolsheviks. The mood in the social democratic masses of Petrograd is going to the left. In this connection the Petrograd elections only confirm those facts, already known to us earlier; the ousting of the Mensheviks by the Bolsheviks in the factory committees, in the district party organisations, the conquest of the trade unions by the Bolsheviks, the victories of Bolshevik-Internationalist resolutions* [ie Bolshevik and left wing Menshevik] *over Menshevik ones in the Soviet of Workers' and Soldiers' deputies.*[129]

Coming a month later the Moscow urban elections demonstrated the further radicalism produced by the Kornilov coup and the intensifying crisis. On the one hand, the Cadets' relative position was strengthened as their absolute vote barely diminished. But on the left the Menshevik vote slumped relatively and fell absolutely from 81,000 to 16,000—a fall of 80 percent. The Socialist Revolutionary vote collapsed even more spectacularly from 360,000 to 55,000—an absolute fall of almost 85 percent. The Bolshevik vote by contrast rose from 12 to 51 percent and absolutely from 184,000 to 194,000. By continuing the analysis beyond October to include the results for the Constituent Assembly elections held in the November (based on a massive turnout) this basic pattern can be confirmed.

In the countryside too support was dissolving rapidly for the SRs, 'while local militants in the *uezd* and *guberniia* peasant committees and soviets were still inclined to stick to the party line, the patience of the peasants themselves was running out and direct action coming to the fore... The chiefs were allowing themselves to be transformed into the main prop of authority at the local level'.[130] Viewed in these terms the Constituent Assembly results were no fluke in being an overwhelming left vote with the Bolsheviks gaining 25 percent and a clear victory in the industrial areas and key fronts in the army—a result all the more impressive if the balance between the right SR and left SR vote is properly understood as we will try to show in a moment.

Thus the better known swing away from the SRs and Mensheviks in the soviets and factory committees was a reflection of a much wider trend clearly apparent in the local government elections in the two biggest cities. Since a discussion of the trend in the committees and soviets can easily be found elsewhere we will here simply draw attention to Table 3 which shows the changing position in the first three All-Russian Congresses of Soviets

Once again the swing to the Bolsheviks is evident. Secondly, the weakening appeal of both the SRs and the Mensheviks is clearly apparent reflecting what Read terms 'their refusal to go along with their constituents'.[132] Thirdly, we can see that within these parties the centre right weakened, producing a much more even balance with the left in the delegates of the Mensheviks and SRs at the Second Congress. The left SRs formed a separate party after the Second Congress, ensuring their domination of SR support at the Third Congress. Behind these figures lay a complex process of division and weakening in both the SRs and the Mensheviks. If, as we have argued, the revolutionary upsurge remade the Bolshevik Party and pushed it towards revolution, its impact on the SRs and Mensheviks was the opposite—parts of the parties began to split and move towards counter-revolution while the mainstream equivocated before drifting into opposition.

The internal divisions and weakening of the SRs

As we have seen, the Socialist Revolutionaries were the biggest party on the left. Their initial success was based on the combination of an appeal to the towns with socialist demands and an appeal to the peasants based

TABLE 2: PERCENT DISTRIBUTION OF VOTE IN PETROGRAD AND MOSCOW DUMA AND CONSTITUENT ASSEMBLY ELECTIONS[128]

	Petrograd 27-29 May	Petrograd 20 August	Petrograd November	Moscow 25 June	Moscow 24 September	Moscow November
Cadet	21.9	20.9	26.2	18.0	26.6	34.5
Minor-non socialist	1.3	1.4	6.9	0.2	2.8	—
Socialist bloc (mainly SR)	44.2	37.4	16.1	56.2	14.4	8.1
Socialist Revolutionaries	7.4					4.6
Minor socialist	1.4	2.6	2.2	1.5	1.2	—
Mensheviks	3.4	4.3	3.1	12.6	4.1	2.8
Bolsheviks	20.4	33.4	45.0	11.5	50.9	47.9
Other	—	—	—	—	—	2.0
TOTAL VOTERS	784,910	549,350	942,333	640,142	379,639	764,763

on support for their right to have the land. In the spring of 1917 this enabled the SRs to dwarf other parties with a membership of at least half a million and possibly many more, grouped in 60 province organisations as well as organisations in the army and fleet. By the summer membership may even have gone as high as a million as whole villages and army units joined up.

But the Socialist Revolutionaries were always loosely organised and disparate, divided by the war and then split wide apart in 1917 itself. Although to some extent an oversimplification, three tendencies resulted—a right, centre and left. The right was led by Kerensky, Breshkovskaya and Savinikov grouping politically around the paper *Volia naroda*. The centre, until the summer the dominant force, was led by Victor Chernov. But from the spring a left Socialist Revolutionary group developed, grouped around the *Novy put* and *Znamya truda* journals and led by Spiridonova, Natanson and Kamkov. The growing isolation of the right *within* the party was reflected in the way in June Kerensky was excluded from the central committee and, after the failure of the Kornilov coup, Savinikov was expelled. From the other side Chernov, removed from his position as minister of agriculture, in part as a concession to property owners, also felt free to attack the Provisional government and the right even more in September 1917.

But the main beneficiaries of this disillusion were not so much the centre as the left Socialist Revolutionaries. In September 1917 they won control of the Petrograd committee of the party and as popular support haemorrhaged the left looked set to gain control of the party as a whole in the autumn. What the left SRs lacked, however, was control of the party apparatus and when October came Chernov and the centre effectively sunk their differences with the right using their control of the party to oppose the taking of power and drive out the left SRs who, though they could not command the leading organs, clearly had a mass of support in the base of the party. When the left SRs decided to stay in the Second Congress of Soviets, the central committee of the party expelled the 79 who remained. Then on 11 November the Extraordinary Congress of Peasant Soviets met in Petrograd with some 195 left SR delegates against around 65 right and centre SRs. Even if there are doubts about particular mandates this shows the massive swing that had taken place.

This Congress too voted to support the revolution and the left SRs formed a party of their own on 24 November, joining the Bolsheviks to create a revolutionary coalition. When the full Second Congress of Peasant Deputies met on 26 November with roughly 350 Left SR delegates against some 300 centre and Right SRs (and around 90

TABLE 3: PERCENT DISTRIBUTION OF DELEGATES TO FIRST THREE CONGRESSES OF SOVIETS BY PARTY AND PARTY TENDENCY [131]

CONGRESS	BOLSHEVIK	SOCIALIST REVOLUTIONARY			MENSHEVIK		OTHER	NON-PARTY
		Left SR	Maximalist SR	Centre right SR	Menshevik Internationalist	Centre right Menshevik		
FIRST (3 June)	13	—	—	34.5	4	33	8.5	6
SECOND (25 October)	52	15	—	13	7	7	1.4	4
THIRD (10 January 1918)	53	21	1.7	3.2	2.1	2.1	1.2	15

Bolsheviks) Spiridonova, the leader of the Left SRs, defeated Chernov to be elected chair. He immediately took the Right and centre SRs out of the Congress to try to create a parallel body. Far from embodying a superior claim to 'democracy', the mainstream leadership of the SRs were only able to act as they did by manipulating their control of the party.

The elections for the Constituent Assembly merely enabled them to take this manipulation a step further. Although historians hostile to the revolution dwell on the fact that the SRs were the largest party, they neglect the absence of evidence that the position espoused by its leadership had real support beyond the top echelons. The SR electoral list had been drawn up before the full impact of the polarisation to the left outside and within the party. The list therefore gave an enormous preponderance to the Right and the centre to such an extent that when some 420 SRs were elected only around 40 of them were from the Left. As the analysis above should make clear, this in no sense represented the true balances of forces during the last days in which the SR party was united. But the SR leadership had no qualms about seizing this further opportunity to weaken the revolutionary front in favour of its failed policy of compromise.

When the Constituent Assembly was so casually disbanded its obvious lack of mass support exposed the SRs claim to have a mass popular base to legitimate their obstruction of the new government. The Constituent Assembly, with effective SR dominance, in its limited life refused to endorse the government's policy on land, even though this was to all intents the historic policy of the SRs. This demonstrates the impasse to which the party had come and how Chernov and other centre left leaders had allowed it to be marginalised in their support of the chimera of some wider class compromise in 1917.

The internal divisions and weakening of the Mensheviks

Similar processes of division could be found within the smaller Menshevik Party in the summer and autumn. Figures of party membership remain uncertain partly because of the chaotic state of party organisations in 1917 and partly because in the peripheral areas Menshevik and Bolshevik groups sometimes remained united during 1917, occasionally splitting only after October. Miller suggests that a realistic evaluation of the comparative dynamics of Bolshevik and Menshevik membership shows the Bolsheviks with some 10,000 members in February rising to 40,000 by the time of their April conference and around 200,000 in the summer. By October he accepts the traditional figure of some 350,000 members. In comparison the Mensheviks grew much faster early on—to some 100,000 in April. A rough equality was reached in August with the Mensheviks having around 200,000 members but then in the remaining months they failed to grow any more. Their relative weakness was also reflected in their heavy dependence for members on areas like the Caucuses (around 50,000 members in Georgia alone) whereas the Bolsheviks dominated the industrial heartlands of Russia. The Mensheviks also had a weaker proportional working class base and drew fewer workers into positions of leadership. Whereas at the summer 1917 conference of the Bolshevik Party some 40 percent of delegates were workers, in the Menshevik conference the figure was closer to 20 percent. This was partly related to the party's failure to focus to the same extent as the Bolsheviks, or in some instances the SRs, on working class issues. Many years ago, for example, Ward pointed out that coverage of the factory committee movement was better in the SR paper, *Delo naroda,* than Menshevik papers and the main Menshevik paper in Petrograd did not even discuss the May-June Factory Committee Conference in the city.[133]

The Mensheviks, like the SRs, had three main tendencies. On the right, led by Postresov, were those who had supported the war before and after February—the so called Defencists. These were few in number—at the Menshevik conference in August they had the support of only around 5 percent of delegates—but they were a powerful influence on those who participated in the Provisional government and those who supported participation. By August around 55 percent of members supported the centre—the so called Revolutionary Defencists, led by Mikhail Liber and Fedor Dan. Around 30 percent supported the party's left wing (with another 10 percent supporting a United Social Democratic-Internationalist strand) amongst whom Martov was the leading figure although his personal influence in the party at large was much wider. Moreover it was in the 'Bolshevik belt' (as Larin described it in September 1917) of industrial Russia that the Menshevik Internationalist wing was the stronger part of the party reflecting the way that the base of the party was being pulled to the left.[134]

The Menshevik leadership's difficulties presented an obvious problem. If they had the correct analysis why was the working class turning away from them? Their answer was crassly reductionist. Real class conscious workers, they argued, supported their more moderate position. Therefore those who did not support them could not be class conscious workers but were instead socially less stable groups including a mass of soldiers. Indeed Postresov had earlier prefigured this argument claiming that truly class conscious workers would have supported the war effort and working class opposition to the war was therefore a manifestation of its social dilution. Later Martov, who saw Postresov's view as absurd, found himself caught up in the same reductionist logic on an even larger scale arguing that the post-war wave of radicalism across the Western world—'world Bolshevism' was a reflection of a war-induced dilution of the Western working class including the influx of women untrained in the class struggle.[135]

The trouble was that even their own members felt this pressure in October. In Petrograd on 24 October, as the Mensheviks in Pre-Parliament had some last minute success in forcing it into a more oppositional stance to the Provisional government, they could not even call demonstrations to support their pressure on Kerensky least the demonstrators reflected Bolshevik ideas.[136]

The issue of power

When the third coalition government was announced on 25 September the Petrograd Soviet immediately passed a motion which read:

> *We, the workers and garrison of Petrograd will give no support whatsoever to a government of bourgeois omnipotence and counter-revolutionary coercion. We express our complete assurance that the news of the new government will meet with one answer alone from all the revolutionary democracy, 'Resign!' And, basing our actions on this unified voice of true democracy, the All-Russian Congress of Workers' and Soldiers' Deputies, will create a true revolutionary power.* [137]

The prediction was correct. When the Second Congress convened, there were some 670 delegates from 400 soviets, including 300 Bolsheviks, some 200 SRs of whom around half were Left SRs and 33 Menshevik Internationalists. As the delegates began to convene they were asked their views on the question of power. Table 4 sets out the results.

TABLE 4: VIEWS OF THE DELEGATES TO THE SECOND CONGRESS OF SOVIETS ON GOVERNMENT[138]

For 'All power to the soviets'	505
For 'All power to democracy'	86
For a democratic coalition without Cadets	21
For a democratic coalition with the Cadets	58

Thus only 79 delegates were prepared to consider a coalition with the bourgeoisie and only 58 with the only serious bourgeois party.

It can be argued, therefore, that had the Bolsheviks not played the role they did in October in pushing for a decisive response to what was seen as the continuing hesitations of the Provisional government, there would still have been a push for power from below. On the Military Revolutionary Committee, for example, although the Bolsheviks played a leading role they had only 53 out of some 80 members and the remaining 27 were by no means less militant.

In fact, as we know with hindsight, the seizure of power in Petrograd on 24-25 October was easy because the Provisional government no longer had support. 'When a power was not defended by those who organised it—was it needed?' asked Malyantovich, the last minister of justice in the Provisional government.[139] The Second Congress of Soviets met on 25 October, after revolutionary workers, troops and Red Guards had seized the key centres of power in Petrograd. But with the outcome still uncertain, the Socialist Revolutionary and Menshevik leaderships now had to cease equivocating and respond. Dan, for the Mensheviks, predictably still proposed an homogenous democratic coalition. Martov went further, calling for a socialist coalition and this call generated support from both the Left SRs and the Bolsheviks and was approved unanimously. At this point the representatives of the main Menshevik groups turned on the Congress and the new leadership denouncing them and walking out with the right SRs and Bundists, leaving Martov plaintively echoing his call for unity with those who had left. The situation was now different. 'We all accepted Martov's proposal to discuss peaceful ways of solving the crisis,' said Lunarcharsky, '...but a systematic attack was launched at us... Without hearing us out, *without even discussing their own proposals*, they immediately tried to separate themselves from us...to isolate us'.[140] Having had the ground pulled from under him by his own comrades, Martov was then forced to choose between the Congress and his party. Fatally he abandoned the Congress leaving with most of the rest of the Menshevik Internationalists to what Trotsky famously called 'the dustbin of history'.

The popular movement

The devaluation of the political choices made in 1917 extends in another direction, as we suggested earlier. This is the direction of the political choice made by the workers. In some analyses it is as if revolutionary ideas float above the working class—in the Bolshevik Party—until workers, driven by the pressure of events, converged with the Bolsheviks in October. Any serious account of radicalisation has to give prominence to the real forces affecting the development of the popular movement. But there is an additional political dimension to radicalisation that also needs to be incorporated but rarely has been. Politics is there in the way in which the individuals who made up the popular movement made choices between alternatives, formed in the context of political debates, however poorly or inarticulately they were formulated. Yet in some accounts it is almost as if workers, faced with growing pressure, were the subject of blind forces which drove them towards the Bolshevik Party in the autumn of 1917.

Suny unwittingly expresses this view when he writes that 'by early fall 1917 a *coincidence* of lower class aspiration and the Bolshevik programme resulted in elected *Leninist* majorities in the soviets of both Petrograd and Moscow and the strategic support of soldiers on the Northern and Western fronts.' Read goes further still arguing that 'the popular agenda—a better deal for workers, land redistribution, protection from economic crisis, greater direct democracy and a just end to the war—remained a relatively stable programme in search of implementation' and that the workers only turned to the Bolsheviks because neither the SRs or the Mensheviks would carry out this programme, concluding that 'the popular movement did not turn towards Bolshevism because they became converts to its basic philosophy'.[141]

But even were this completely true, workers' actions would still involve a double political choice. There was the choice of the established parties that we have already noted. There was the political judgement that workers then made (and which they had not made earlier) that these parties were no longer to be trusted and that the Bolsheviks were a better guarantee of their aspirations would be realised. Ignoring this political element creates an account that converges with that offered by Menshevik theorists in the autumn and winter of 1917. According to this the 'coincidence' of interest between the popular movement and the Bolsheviks was based on no more than a temporary conjuncture. The Bolsheviks should have understood this and rejected power. For their part the 'socialist' opposition to taking power in October was justified in opposing it since a gap was bound to open up as the popular movement fell away. At this point the Bolsheviks' opponents could say, 'We told you so,' and reap the benefit of their stand. Even worse, the devaluation of politics lends support to those like Pipes, Figes and many modern historians in Russia who, in their different ways, see the social movement as a mob. Whether intentionally or not these historians therefore allow themselves to play a trick which devalues the need to explore and understand the nature of political commitment in 1917, implicitly legitimises the anti-Bolshevik position on the left in 1917 and then removes the need to explore how the actions of the anti-Bolshevik parties during and after October might themselves have contributed to the problems of trying to stabilise the revolution.

The difficulty with their argument is threefold. The first problem is what the Bolsheviks were doing during 1917. Sukhanov in an oft quoted passage writes that they were 'at the factory benches and in the barracks every blessed day. For the masses, they had became their own people, because they were always there.' Did this mean that they were standing there like some mute magnetic pole of attraction drawing inert iron filings towards them? Of course this was not the case. They were there winning and losing arguments, selling or failing to sell their newspapers, successfully or unsuccessfully collecting money, carrying or failing to convince the people over political issues. And their opponents, less often present, if Sukhanov is correct, were doing exactly the same when they were there. Secondly, to the extent that workers made a pro-revolutionary choice we can argue that this was a better political choice than that made by their leaders who were abandoning them. The argument that the revolution had to go forward made sense in terms of the experience that workers were having. It made sense in terms of what at other times might disparagingly be called the 'low politics' of their everyday lives. Conventional politics, of course, is high politics, conducted from afar with human beings as its subjects. In 1917, however, high politics became 'low politics' just because the political process could no longer be contained in palaces, chancelleries and parliaments. And finally, put in these terms, the onus is thrown back on those whose politics, at the crucial moment, led them to stand aside or oppose the popular movement. As in any social conflict, to stand aside at the crucial moment is perhaps to live to fight another day but it is also to weaken your side, perhaps fatally.[142]

Compounding the error

Accounts of the October Revolution too often end with Lenin standing in the Second Congress of Soviets late on the night of 25 October 1917. In fact the revolution was a process which began in Petrograd on 24-25 October but continued over several months as it spread across Russia. In the spring the problem of consolidating the revolution merged with the brief but spectacular advance of the German armies which forced the Treaty of Brest-Litovsk. Then a couple of months later it merged with the beginning of the civil war. Soviet accounts dealing with this as 'the triumphal march' of Soviet power made a nonsense of the complex problems that consolidating power entailed. Apart from the important issue of the continuing dynamic of the revolution from below, analysing the consolidation of the revolution also requires attention to the policies of the SRs and Mensheviks after the October events in Petrograd. Since the pattern of response was set in the first few days, we will conclude our discussion by setting out how these new divisions confirmed the choices made on 24-25 October.

Few historians have resisted the temptation to treat the emergency measures of the first months of Soviet power as the outcome of imminent tendencies in Bolshevism or opportunistic volte faces from earlier positions held. But it is here that what is traditionally seen as the historians' question of 'what happened next?' becomes important. Much of the recent history of the revolution has been written in terms of the deeper structures which help to determine historical events. But this does not mean that the history of events can be ruled out completely and even less that 'events' are predetermined by structure.Things happen one after another as contexts and problems change and then a grasp of chronology and movement becomes crucial. This is even more so in a revolution because the speed of events accelerates. Bukharin put this well just before the October events:

> In a time of revolution with its inevitable ebb and flow of the tide, when, like in the cinema, the situation, historical picture, faces, figures change quickly and events scarcely allow one to keep hold of oneself, it is completely natural that institutions, developing at the beginning of this violent historical tornado, repeatedly change their role and significance. [143]

The immediate consolidation of the revolution in Petrograd faced three explicitly counter-revolutionary challenges—the military opposition outside the city; a threat from officers inside the city and a strike of white collar employees designed to prevent the state apparatus being taken over. In addition, the Mensheviks and SRs who had left the Congress of Soviets then grouped with others opposed to the revolution (including Cadets) in a Committee for the Salvation of the Revolution and the Motherland. The left wing of this committee was close to the left in the soviets while the centre and right had contacts with those prepared to fight against the revolution. The problem was further complicated by the equivocation of the leadership of the railway workers' union over whether it should support the revolution or not, with its inclination being to draw back from the most radical measures.

It needs to be stressed at this point that neither Lenin, nor Trotsky, nor the Bolsheviks as a whole wanted an all-Bolshevik government to emerge from the taking of power. Indeed tensions in the Bolshevik Party led some who feared isolation to temporarily resign from the party in early November. Why then did a coalition not emerge? Swain, following the tendency of recent historians to endorse the position taken by the SRs and the Mensheviks, has argued:

> ...that the successful campaign to discredit the third Coalition Government and overthrow it within the parliamentary atmosphere of the 'Pre-Parliament' did not result in the formation of a democratic coalition was the fault of the

Bolshevik Party—Lenin…succeeded in seizing power not from the bourgeoisie and the liberals, but from democracy, and its dominant voice, the SR party. [144]

In fact the Committee for the Salvation of the Revolution immediately reproduced all of the divisions about political power that had been apparent on 24 October and before. Should the opposition unite with bourgeois forces against the revolution? Should it be a 'socialist opposition' against both the Bolsheviks and the bourgeoisie and for what? Should it defend the Provisional government (and Kerensky?) or look for a new government that was neither Bolshevik nor from the old Provisional government?

While many on the left which grouped around the committee argued that by forcing the issue of power the Bolsheviks had opened the way for a later counter-revolution, Postresov argued that the seizure of power was the counter-revolution and therefore there could be no compromise with it. It had to be opposed by the socialist opposition uniting with the bourgeoisie (effectively to defend the bourgeois limits of the revolution). Martov, equivocated—seemingly far more concerned not to lose contact with the right wing of the Mensheviks than the Bolsheviks and the soviet. It is symptomatic of the political confusion in the committee that when on 29 October a group of officers and cadets staged an unsuccessful rising in Petrograd they did so under the flag of the committee and with the support of some of its SR and Menshevik members.

What crystallised these problems was the action of the railway workers' union. The executive of the union (VIKZHEL) tried to push all sides back into talks (supporting its position with the threat of a railway strike) about a new coalition government which effectively meant negotiations between the Bolsheviks, the Left SRs and their representatives in the Second Congress of Soviets, the centre Menshevik and SR leadership and those forces grouped around the Committee for Salvation.

Despite Swain's argument that the Bolsheviks were responsible for the failure of these talks the evidence points in the opposite direction, including that which he quotes in his account. When negotiations began the Menshevik and SR leaders immediately demanded a coalition which would *exclude* the Bolsheviks, despite the talks being aimed at an all-socialist coalition. On 28 October the union reported to its Moscow headquarters that 'the Bolsheviks are making concessions…the Committee for Salvation is irreconcilable; but we will exert pressure on it'. The next day Gendelman, who had led the SRs out of the Congress of Soviets, rejected the participation of the Bolsheviks in a coalition telling the Committee for Salvation that 'even in the democratic camp there are moments when it is necessary to decide an agreement with weapons.' No comment could have been more unfortunate for the right because that same day officers and cadets in Petrograd staged their insurrection under the flag of the committee. The railway union was therefore forced to condemn the right and those who toyed with them from the centre as 'the madmen who at this moment...do not want compromise. Instead of striving for a compromise, the right part of democracy...put to the Bolsheviks the impossible demand of total capitulation, quite unconcerned for the consequences.'

Under pressure from the union and groups of workers the debate then moved to the possibility of a coalition which would include both right wing socialists and Bolsheviks but not Lenin and Trotsky, with Chernov, the SR leader, as prime minister. From the point of view of the centre right the attraction of this was that it might split the Bolsheviks and allow their influence to be diminished. Not surprisingly therefore the proposal provoked sharp differences within the Bolshevik leadership as their negotiators inclined to support it. But before anyone had a chance to respond part of the right wing of the SR's and the right of the Mensheviks broke away arguing that there could be no compromise and that the revolution had to be opposed. While the Bolsheviks were debating the issue the central committee of the SRs also broke off leaving only a rump in which the Menshevik leaders were prominent. As their own side of the coalition dissolved, undercutting the whole basis of the negotiations, their hopes were briefly raised by the appearance of a split at the top of the Bolshevik Party as a leading group resigned for fear of the revolution being isolated if a compromise was not reached. Dan even boasted, 'Thanks to our tactics, the Bolsheviks are already splitting'.[145]

Against this Lenin and Trotsky argued that any coalition had to recognise the shift in power that had occurred and allow the Bolsheviks a leading role. Power could no longer hang in the air or between competing institutions, it had to be based in the soviets, the Bolsheviks had to be a major part of any coalition and the presence of Lenin and Trotsky themselves was important not for personal reasons but as a reflection of agreement that something significant had changed. A coalition which dropped the leaders of the major party was a nonsense. 'Nothing whatever can come of merely leaving a few Bolsheviks in a coalition government,' said Trotsky; 'We have taken power—and we must also bear the responsibilities'.[146]

The talks crumbled not because of an objection in principle to a socialist coalition on the part of the Bolshevik leadership but because the SRs and the Mensheviks were not prepared to negotiate a meaningful coalition *and* because, as they prevaricated, their own side was falling apart. In the short term this had two consequences. Those members of the Bolshevik leadership quickly returned, chastened, to the fold. Secondly, the process of break-up of the SR party was hastened with the Left SRs forming a new revolutionary coalition government with the Bolsheviks and against their former comrades. It was this revolutionary coalition that would take the revolution through its first months before it was split by entirely different issues in the spring of 1918.

Now isolated, the old SR leadership and the Mensheviks looked to the Constituent Assembly and beyond to establish a third force which they imagined would allow them to stand between the revolution and the bourgeoisie. In so doing they merely built on their past errors. Although it had not been apparent in October, it was increasingly clear that the basis of the Constituent Assembly and the soviets was a competing and not a complementary one. This is why the right now put so much emphasis on the Constituent Assembly. The Cadet Nabokov, for example, now argued on the eve of elections that he had not wanted, occurring at a time he had opposed, with an electorate he despised, that 'it is necessary to hold the elections whenever there is the slightest possibility of doing so. The gravest responsibility towards the country will be insured by all who dare to cast doubt on the correctness of the elections of the Constituent Assembly on which the whole country is henceforth setting its hopes'.[147]

Although the swing to the Bolsheviks and Left SRs was continuing post-October it was clear that the united SR ticket was going to emerge as the major force in any assembly because of the huge peasant vote. But the SR leadership could only interpret this as a vote for stability if they ignored the split in the SR party and the further radicalisation of the peasantry. Beyond this the party complexion was to an extent irrelevant since the majority of delegates elected to the Constituent Assembly were clearly elected by a population voting for peace, for land redistribution, a transfer of power to the workers and, in many areas, self determination. The Constituent Assembly could only prevent this if it became the basis of yet another government that would rule over the people. As Bukharin had put it, in a revolution the film moves faster and institutions and parties change their role: the Constituent Assembly, once the symbol of revolutionary progress, was now the symbol of something else. But the ultimate fate of the revolution would now be decided by how a much bigger question was answered.

In the period 1917 to 1921 the Bolsheviks would undoubtedly make many mistakes but they would make them against a background of a revolutionary opportunity in the West that could have helped them but was missed. There, revolutionary crises were pushed to the brink but there was no Bolshevik Party to respond. The socialist equivalents of the SRs and the Mensheviks held out against revolution and assisted consciously or unconsciously in the process by which the crisis was diffused. In 1921 they could look proudly at their handiwork. The crisis had been successfully negotiated in the West, and in Russia, though victorious in the civil war, the Bolsheviks were weakened enormously, the working class destroyed and the remnants of the revolution isolated. But their success was an illusion. A year later in Italy Mussolini came to power, then in 1933 Hitler came to power in Germany. In both East and West there was a high price to pay for the failure of international revolution.

Already in the summer of 1917, *before October*, a writer in the *Spartakus* journal in Germany argued, 'Here begins the fatal destiny of the Russian Revolution. The dictatorship of the proletariat in Russia is destined to suffer a desperate defeat compared to which the fate of the Paris Commune was child's play—unless the international proletarian revolution gives it support in time.' Whoever wrote this could not have foreseen that in Russia the defeat of the revolution would take the form of Stalin's counter-revolution but he saw the essence of the problem. So too did Rosa Luxemburg. She did not fear to criticise what she thought were the mistakes the Bolsheviks might be making but she also saw where the blame would lie if they failed. Writing to Luise Kautsky from prison in 1917 she saw something else:

> Are you happy about the Russians? Of course, they will not be able to main-tain themselves in this witches' sabbath, not because some statistics show economic development in Russia to be too backward as your clever husband has figured out, but because social democracy in the highly developed West consists of miserable and wretched cowards who will look quietly on and let the Russians bleed to death.[148]

Notes

1   Readers unfamiliar with the argument about the movement from below in both Russia and Europe can be recommended two excellent review articles, D Howl, 'The Russian Revolution', *International Socialism* 62, Spring, 1994; D Gluckstein, 'Revolution and the Challenge of Labour', *International Socialism* 61, Winter 1993.

2   O Figes, *A People's Tragedy. The Russian Revolution 1891-1924* (Cape, 1996) is the latest attempt to rewrite the history of the revolution. The ideas criticised here permeate this discussion so that capitalism and the ruling class almost disappear from his account as social forces.

3   Not all right wing accounts view Tsarist Russia optimistically. Martin Malia argues that 'it would have required a near miracle for Russia to have evolved organically and peacefully into a constitutional democracy had she been spared the shock of the First World War.' But he then argues that the most likely scenario was a failed revolution producing a 'national conservative regime' which would have created an authoritarian regime (like Franco's Spain) preferable to the totalitarianism which he believes did result from 1917. M Malia, *The Soviet Tragedy: A History of Socialism in Russia 1917-1991* (Free Press, 1994).

4   This relative weakness is confirmed by the work of Paul Gregory who has reconstructed Russian national income from the Tsarist data itself. Gregory has recently offered himself as a historian whose work lends encouragement to the view that market capitalism can transform the prospects of modern Russia. But his

figures of long run growth per head show that Russia simply did not grow faster than advanced Western Europe and therefore could not have been on a convergence path. Nor does it help to extrapolate from Russia's highest pre-1914 period of growth since on his own admission this was shorter than equivalent periods in other countries. P Gregory, *Russian National Income 1885-1913* (Cambridge University Press, 1982).

5   C Read, *From Tsar to Soviets. The Russian People and their Revolution, 1917-1921* (UCL Press, 1996), p34. Although we will later suggest some problems with Read's account it is much to be preferred to Figes' account. Unfortunately it has not received the same attention as Figes' repudiation of the revolution.

6   The idea of patrimonialism is summed up in a sentence of Tsar Nicholas II: 'I conceive of Russia as a landed estate of which the proprietor is the Tsar, the administrator is the nobility and the workers are the peasantry.'

7   Quoted in R Pipes, *Struve: Liberal on the Right, 1905-1944* (Harvard University Press, 1980), p175.

8   G Freeze, 'The Soslovie Paradigm and Russian Social History', *American Historical Review*, vol 91 no 1, 1986; L Haimson, 'The Problem of Social Identities in Early 20th Century Russia', *Slavic Review*, vol 47 (1988).

9   Thus the idea, argued in different ways by Perry Anderson, Tom Nairn and Arno Mayer (and going back to Joseph Schumpeter and beyond) that the aristocracy remained the dominant force in Europe in 1914 because it had contained and 'feudalised' the bourgeoisie can be stood on its head. The aristocracy remained a powerful force precisely because key sections of it had adapted to capitalism, becoming subject to 'embourgeoisement' where it mattered.

10   The best study is A J Reiber, *Merchants and Entrepreneurs in Imperial Russia* (Chapel Hill, 1982).

11   Quoted in M Ferro, *Nicholas II The Last of the Tsars* (Viking 1991), p200.

12   Quoted in R Pipes, op cit, p177.

13   K Kautsky, *The Driving Forces and Prospects of the Russian Revolution*. This pamphlet was widely translated in Russia after 1905.

14   See P Miliukov, *Political Memoirs 1905-1917* (University of Michigan Press, 1967), pp287-288, 308-309.

15   Quoted in R Pipes, op cit, pp73, 210-218.

16   R H Johnson, *Tradition Versus Revolution. Russia and the Balkans in 1917* (Columbia University Press, 1977), p172.

17   D Geyer, *Russian Imperialism. The Interaction of Domestic and Foreign Policy, 1860-1914* (Berg, 1987), p255. Geyer points out that the failure to develop a specific theory of imperialism applied to Russia before 1917 leads to Russian expansion being seen as 'a natural law of Russian history'. In its place he offers an approach largely in terms of the model of social imperialism developed by German historians like Wehler and Fischer: 'internal tensions' were 'deflected' outwards into imperial conquest and the fulfilment of 'traditional desires' in conflicts with 'ancient enemies' (p345-346). This approach is illuminating, but as in German historiography, can be misleading if it becomes the whole story since it underplays economic interests and fails to locate the more 'modern' capitalist drives behind expansion. See D Blackbourn and G Eley, *The Peculiarities of German History: Bourgeois Society and Politics in Nineteenth Century Germany* (Oxford University Press, 1984).

18   'Imperialism' is frequently confused with 'colonialism'. The Marxist theory of imperialism was developed to explain the expansive clash of state power in the heartland of capitalism in 1914 not the scramble for Africa or anywhere else. For a brief review of Russia's great power role see P Struve, 'The Balkan War and Russia's Task', *The Russian Review*, vol 2 no 2, May 1913, pp11-13. See also R Pipes, op cit, pp88-97, 180-186, 201-210, 216, 243.

19   N Stone, *The Eastern Front* (Hodder & Stoughton, 1975), p285.
20   Quoted in V V Shelokhaev (ed), *Politicheskaya istoriya Rossii v partiyakh i litsakh* (Moscow, 1993), pp101-102.
21   The best account remains N Stone, op cit.
22   Sir B Pares, *Russia* (Penguin, 1941), pp88-89.
23   Quoted V S Daikin, 'The Leadership Crisis in Russia on the Eve of the February Revolution', *Voprosy istorii no.3* 1982, translated in *Studies in Soviet History*, vol xxiii no 1, Summer 1984.
24   W Rosenberg, *Liberals in the Russian Revolution. The Constitutional Democratic Party, 1917-1921* (Princeton University Press, 1974), pp43-45.
25   Quoted V V Shelokhaev, op cit, p295.
26   C Read, op cit, p44; Guchkov quoted in Shelokhaev, op cit, p296.
27   Sometimes this was brought home personally to the politicians. As he was on the way to help resolve the crisis at the top the Cadet constitutionalist Nabokov recalled being stopped by a man in the street who told him, 'Do not leave any Romanovs, we have no use for them.' V D Medlin and S L Parsons (eds), *V D Nabokov and the Russian Provisional government, 1917* (Yale, 1974), pp42-43.
28   B I Kolonitskii, 'Anti-bourgeois propaganda and anti-"Burzhui" consciousness in 1917', *The Russian Review*, vol 53, April 1994, pp183-196.
29   'While the three of us—Nabokov, Miliukov and myself—were pondering how to enlist the promulgation of Grand Duke Mikhail's abdication of the throne…we were interrupted by telegrams about sailors executing admirals and officers in Sveaborg and Kronstadt.' wrote Baron Nol'de. It is fortunate that two of the major insider memoirs of the formation of the Provisional government are translated in the same volume, V D Medlin and S L Parsons (eds), op cit. Nabokov was the legal expert of the Cadets. The volume includes two memoirs by him, 'The Provisional government' and 'The Bolshevik coup d'État', and a third by B E Nol'de, who was effectively his assistant, 'V D Nabokov in 1917'. They will be referred to separately below. The quotation from Nol'de is on p16.
30   P Miliukov, op cit, p406. Miliukov's memoirs contain his own thoughts on the problem of the legitimacy of the Provisional government.
31   When L'vov mentioned that he had a mass of telegrams of support for the Provisional government Steklov replied 'We could show you right now far more, ten times as many, telegrams endorsed by hundreds and thousands of organised citizens, which demand that we take power into our own hands.' V D Nabokov, 'The Provisional government', op cit, p125.
32   The fourth Duma elected in 1912 included in its 436 members 150 anti-Semitic far right members, 130 Octobrists and their allies, 55 Cadets, a mere 20 representatives of the national minorities, and some 13 social democrats and 9 Trudoviks representing the mass of peasants and workers.
33   P Miliukov, op cit, p.391.
34   V D Nabokov, 'The Provisional government', op cit, pp.49-53.
35   B E Nol'de, op cit, p20.
36   B E Nol'de, op cit, p20. See V D Nabokov's almost identical formulation, 'The Provisional government', op cit, p53. To maintain this idea of a legitimate transfer of power Nabokov insisted from the start that the essence of February had not been a 'revolution' but a 'coup d'état' since a coup preserves the basis of state power while a revolution might be considered to challenge it.
37   Almost immediately L'vov as head of the Provisional government was forced beyond them when he was pressured into dismissing the heads of the provincial governments of Russia which seemed to confirm that in a constitutional sense February was a revolution and not a coup. Worse from the constitutional perspective on 7 March the Tsar who until then had been technically free was arrested and confined to his Tsarkoe Tselo palace outside Petrograd—a decision

which Nabokov believed confirmed the image of a Tsar being 'dethroned' rather than freely 'abdicating'.

38   R Abraham, *Alexander Kerensky. The First Love of the Revolution* (Sidgwick & Jackson, 1987), pp123-124.

39   R Abraham, op cit, p146.

40   V V Shelokhaev, op cit, p105, gives the figure of over 100; W Rosenberg's study of urban council elections in 1917 found 68 different organisations standing including 9 religious groups, 24 minor non-socialist groups and 20 nationalist parties; W Rosenberg, 'The Russian Municipal Duma Elections of 1917: a Preliminary Computation of the Returns', *Soviet Studies*, vol xxi (1969), pp131-163.

41   W Rosenberg, *Liberals in the Russian Revolution*, op cit, pp90, 190.

42   By comparison the Trade Industrialists ran slates in 35 percent of towns; the Union of House Owners in half of towns. On the left the Bolsheviks could only manage independent slates in 27 percent of towns though they stood in some others as part of a socialist bloc.

43   O Radkey, *The Elections to the Russian Constituent Assembly of 1917* (Cambridge, Massachusetts, 1950), pp16-21. This is the main source but some minor inaccuracies probably exist because a complete set of official results was never published.

44   The potential national problem of the Cadets was already apparent in 1906 in the first Duma elections when they got 39 percent of the urban vote but only 11 percent in landlord assemblies and 4 percent of the peasant vote. W Rosenberg, *Liberals in the Russian Revolution*, op cit, p27.

45   Local elections took place quickly partly because the Provisional government needed a responsible administrative base and partly because it hoped that the framework of local politics could be conditioned by national control, and therefore if local circumstances put radicals in power they would be constrained by the wider national framework. Russia in 1917 therefore presented the paradox of a political society where at the national level the argument was that elections had to be postponed while at the local municipal level perfectly adequate, if not on occasion model, electoral procedures were in place which built on the Municipal Electoral Statue of 15 April 1917.

46   W Rosenberg, *Liberals in the Russian Revolution*, op cit, p161,164, 166, 188.

47   W Rosenberg 'The Russian Municipal Duma Elections of 1917', op cit.

48   W Rosenberg, *Liberals in the Russian Revolution*, op cit, p.55, 188

49   R P Browder and A Kerensky (eds), *The Russian Provisional government of 1917* (Standford University Press, 1961), p135.

50   R Abraham, op cit, pp148-149.

51   L Kochan, 'Cadet Policy in 1917 and the Constituent Assembly', *Slavonic & East European Review*, vol xiv (1967), pp183-192.

52   W Rosenberg, *Liberals in the Russian Revolution*, op cit, p90, 190.

53   M Philips Price, 'In the First All-Russian Congress of Soviets', in M Jones (ed), *Storming the Heavens: Voices of October* (Zwan, 1987), p28; A Kerensky, 'The Provisional government 1917', *Slavonic Review* 1930, p2.

54   L Erwin Heenan, *Russian Democracy's Fatal Blunder: The Summer Offensive of 1917* (Praeger, 1987), is the major attempt to argue this. Her account does contain some useful information but on the central issue she shows a remarkable naivety over the dynamics and constraints which determine the actions of a great power.

55   R A Wade, *The Russian Search For Peace, February-October 1917* (Stanford, 1969), pp143-147.

56   A Kerensky, op cit.

57   Quoted R Abraham, op cit, p341. Russia's declining influence during the war is well brought out by Heenan even though she does do not appear to understand the full implications of this argument. See L E Heenan, pp.3-9.

58   V D Nabokov, 'The Provisional government' op cit, p106.
59   Quoted in G Katkov, *Russia 1917 The Kornilov Affair. Kerensky and the Break-Up of the Russian Army* (Longman, 1980), p14.
60   R Abraham, op cit, pp192-193.
61   V D Nabokov, 'The Provisional government', op cit, p87.
62   V D Nabokov, 'The Provisional government', op cit, p86.
63   *The Times*, 5 January 1918.
64   A Kerensky, op cit, p11.
65   Quoted H Pichter, *Witnesses of the Russian Revolution* (Murray, 1994), pp82-83.
66   A Kerensky, op cit, p9.
67   R A Wade, op cit, pp145-146.
68   See R Abraham, op cit, p278; R A Wade, op cit, pp146-147, on Tereshchenko's negative role; Miliukov approvingly said of Tereshchenko that he 'quietly pursued my very policy and successfully deceived the Soviet of Workers' Deputies', P Miliukov, op cit, p424.
69   Kerensky did not accept the idea of annexations in the west but he had a strong sense of Russia having a role as a great power as well as its civilising mission in the east. See R Abraham, op cit, p12, 99, 174, 237.
70   C Read, op cit, p138; R Abraham, op cit, pp309-310.
71   C Read, op cit, p153 (my emphasis—MH).
72   B Pares, op cit; H Pichter, op cit, p.145. Much of the recent writing on the Russian peasantry has criticised earlier attempts to argue that there was serious class differentiation amongst the peasants. I have a qualified sympathy with this 'revisionism' but to the extent that it is correct it would seem to undercut even more any argument that the rural revolt could have been appeased by anything less than wholesale handover of land to those who worked it.
73   The question of how much land was owned by landlords and others is often shrouded in confusion. For a good contemporary account see L Litoshenko, 'Landed Property in Russia', *Russian Review*, vol 2 no 4, November 1913, pp185-207.
74   It might be objected to this argument that land reform was 'successfully' undertaken at the end of the war in a number of Eastern European countries and was therefore possible in Russia too. But the post-war context of land reform was very different in these countries; so too was the relative power of different sections of the ruling class and the state; but above all concessions were encouraged and minds concentrated by the different experience of Russia.
75   K Tverdovskii [psuedonym. N I Bukharin] 'K voprosy o zemel'nuikh zakhvatakh', *Spartak* no 7, 16 September 1917, reprinted in N I Bukharin, *Na podstupakh k oktyabru, statii i rechi, mai-dekabri 1917 g* (Moscow, 1926), p113.
76   The lack of a wide base of support for private land ownership is also reflected in the fact that formal landowner parties got only 171,245 votes in the elections for the Constituent Assembly.
77   This discussion is based on J Channon, 'The Landowners' in R Sevice (ed), *Society and Politics in the Russian Revolution* (Macmillan) 1992; T V Osipova, 'Vserossiskii soyuz zemel'nykh sobstvennikov v1917g' *Istoriya SSSR* no 3 (1976).
78   C Read, op cit, p118
79   Quoted W Rosenberg, Liberals op cit, p124-125; P Avrich, 'Russian factory committees in 1917', *Jahrbucher fur Geschicte Osteuropas*, 1963, part 2, p167.
80   P Miliukov, op cit, p424.
81   Konovalov became minister of trade and industry; Guchkov was the first minister of war and Tereshchenko, the sugar businessman from the south west, became minister of finance.
82   P Miliukov, op cit, p463; Z Galili, 'Commercial-Industrial Circles in Revolution: the Failure of 'Industrial Progressivism', in E Rogovin, J Frankel, B Knei-Paz

(eds), *Revolution in Russia: Reassessments of 1917* (Cambridge University Press, 1992), p188.

83   The best short summary account of the economic problems of 1917 remains N Stone, op cit, ch 13.

84   Quoted in L Schapiro, *1917: The Russian Revolution and the Origins of Present Day Communism* (Penguin, 1984), p97.

85   W G Rosenberg and D Koenker, *Strikes and Revolution in Russia 1917* (Princeton University Press, 1989).

86   S A Smith, *Red Petrograd: Revolution in the Factories 1917-1918* (Cambridge University Press, 1983), p146.

87   The ambiguity and changing balance of meaning can be seen clearly in the main resolution of the first All-Russian Congress of Factory Committees—easily available in J Reed, *Ten Days that Shook the World* (Penguin, 1966), pp295-296.

88   Z Galili, 'Commercial-Industrial Circles in Revolution: the Failure of 'Industrial Progressivism', op cit, p204.

89   'The Disorganisation of Russian Industry', *Russia: A Journal of Russian-American Trade*, May 1918, pp11-13.

90   L Lande, 'The Mensheviks in 1917', L Haimson (ed), *The Mensheviks from the Revolution of 1917 to the Second World War* (University of Chicago Press, 1976), p41.

91   Quoted H Pichter, op cit, p114.

92   C Read, op cit, p136 ; R Abraham, op cit, p219; P Miliukov, op cit, pp471-472.

93   P Miliukov, op cit, pp464-474; W Rosenberg, *Liberals in the Russian Revolution*, op cit, p198.

94   The most detailed account of the Kornilov coup is by G Katkov, op cit. Katkov combines a detailed command of the sources with a defence of highly questionable arguments. He seeks effectively to defend Kornilov and to condemn Kerensky. Despite the mass of valuable information he offers, his account can be faulted in four key areas, firstly in his desire to defend Kornilov he places the most charitable interpretation on his actions and the least charitable on that of his opponents; secondly, he fails to adequately rebut charges that Kornilov had important meetings with interested groups before the coup; thirdly, and most seriously, he abstracts his account from the social dynamics of the situation and the balance of changing class forces, especially at the top of Russian society; finally, he minimises the role of Allied and especially British involvement which although certainly hesitant was not insignificant. For more politically astute accounts of the coup see J D White, 'The Kornilov Affair—a Study in Counter-Revolution', *Soviet Studies*, vol 20, October 1968, pp187-205; M Ferro, *October 1917: A Social History of the Russian Revolution* (Routledge, 1980); for a survey of the historiography of the coup which criticises Katkov's more narrow interpretation see J W Long, 'Kornilov Redivivus: New Data on the Prelude to Bolshevism', *Russian History*, vol 11 no 1, Spring 1984, pp1-10. Most recently, G Swain, *The Origins of the Russian Civil War* (Longman, 1996), ch 1, is good on the coup.

95   The traditional Russian officer corps was a highly conservative force in Russian society. It celebrated its anti-intellectual stance even in military matters and lacked an appreciation 'that the Russian army's weakness was caused by the backwardness of Russia's society and economy'. A 'young Turk' group had arisen before 1914 but with limited effect. Now the war to some extent democratised the lower ranks but there was still insufficient time for this to penetrate to create the high army structure. See P Kenez, 'Russian Officer Corps Before the Revolution: the Military Mind', *Russian Review* vol 31 (1972), pp226-231; D R Jones, 'The Officers and the October Revolution', *Soviet Studies*, vol xxviii, no 2, April 1976, pp 207-223; and most usefully, A Wildman, 'Officers of the General Staff and the

Kornilov Movement', in E R Frankel, J Frankel and B Knei-Paz (eds), *Revolution in Russia: Reassessments of 1917* (Cambridge University Press, 1992).

96   Quoted G Katkov, op cit, p166.

97   R Abraham, op cit, p227. It is unclear how many soldiers were shot after the restoration of the death penalty. Officially few death penalties were sanctioned at the top but actions may have been taken by local commanders. Kerensky boasted to General Knox that within a week Kornilov had 147 men shot but this may have been said for effect.

98   Quoted in G Katkov, op cit, p169.

99   Quoted in M Leibman, *The Russian Revolution* (Cape,1970), p189.

100 C Read, op cit, p52.

101 Quoted in W Rosenberg, *Liberals in the Russian Revolution*, op cit, p209-210.

102 R Abraham, op cit, p233; G Katkov, op cit, p63.

103 Quoted in V V Shelokhaev, op cit, p316.

104 G Katkov, op cit, p175; G Swain, op cit, ch 1.

105 G Katkov, op cit, pp141, 143; W Rosenberg, *Liberals in the Russian Revolution*, op cit, p223. The same attitude was apparent in the contacts between Allied representatives and the General Headquarters. Buchanan, the British ambassador, clearly would have been happy with a successful coup but felt that he could not be seen to give any open support before the event. He therefore held supporters of a coup at arms length while doing nothing to dissuade it. At the Stavka, on the other hand, the British liaison officer was happy to be swept along by events and to encourage Kornilov.

106 C Read, op cit, p140.

107 Sadly, two of the best social historians of 1917 have retreated towards post-modernism. See S Smith, 'Writing the history of the Russian Revolution After the Fall of Communism', *Europe-Asia Studies*, vol 46 no 4 (1994) pp563-578; R G Suny, 'Revision and Retreat in the Historiography of 1917: Social History and its Critics', *Russian Review*, vol 53, April 1994, pp165-182. For a brief critique see J E Marot, 'A post-modern approach to the Russian Revolution? Comment on Suny', *The Russian Review*, vol 54, April 1995, pp260-264.

108 The directory consisted of Kerensky, Tereshchenko as foreign minister, Verkhovsky and Verderevsky in charge of the war and navy, and Nikitin in charge of posts and telegraphs.

109 So far as I am aware there is no study of the Senate and Duma in 1917 which is unfortunate as they were centres of reaction after February.

110 V D Nabokov, 'The Provisional government', op cit, p78.

111 The conference passed a motion in support of coalition with the bourgeoisie by only 766 to 688 but then rejected the idea of a coalition with the Cadets—the only serious bourgeois party. When the vote for coalition was put a second time it was decisively lost, which Figes ascribes to the way 'the basic skills of parliamentary decision making proved beyond its leaders'; O Figes, op cit, p466. We would explain it more simply in terms of the scale of the polarisation which now existed.

112 Z Galili, *The Menshevik Leaders in the Russian Revolution: Social Realities and Political Strategies* (Princeton University Press, 1989), p389-390.

113 C Read, op cit, p70; S A Smith, op cit.

114 V M Kruchkovskaya, *Tsentral'naya Gorodskaya Duma Petrograda v 1917g* (Moscow, 1986), pp60-63.

115 J Reed, op cit.

116 L Schapiro, op cit, px.

117 V I Lenin, *Collected Works*, vol 26, pp21, 74-77; vol 25, p340; vol 24, p513.

118 On the changing conception of bourgeois revolution in 1917 as it was articulated by the Mensheviks, see L Lande, 'The Mensheviks in 1917', in L Haimson (ed), *The Mensheviks from the Revolution of 1917 to the Second World War* (University

of Chicago Press, 1976), pp15, 17-18, 25-26; B Sapir, 'The Conception of Bourgeois Revolution', ibid, pp366-388

119   L Lande, op cit, p25.
120   N Harding, *Lenin's Political Thought*, vol 2 (London, 1981) p150.
121   B Sapir, op cit, p369.
122   W Rosenberg, *Liberals in the Russian Revolution*, op cit, p250.
123   P Miliukov, op cit, p457-463.
124   V D Nabokov, 'The Bolshevik Coup d'État', op cit, p149-50.
125   *Volia naroda*, 20 September, translated in R P Browder and A Kerensky, op cit, p1641; L Lande, op cit, p29.
126   L Lande, op cit, pp17-19.
127   Z Galili, *The Menshevik Leaders in the Russian Revolution: Social Realities and Political Strategies*, op cit, pp6, 338.
128   W Rosenberg 'The Russian Municipal Duma Elections of 1917', op cit; O Radkey, op cit.
129   *Gordodskoi vestnik vse Rossiiskovo Souza Gorodov*, quoted in V M Kruchkovskaya, op cit, p47.
130   C Read, op cit, p119.
131   Figures do not add up to 100 because of rounding. N N Smirnov, *Tretii Vse Rossiiskii S'ezd Sovetov* (Moscow, 1988) pp.62-63.
132   C Read, op cit, p159.
133   B Ward, 'Wild Socialism in Russia, the Origins', *California Slavic Studies*, vol 3 (1966) p142.
134   I have followed the analysis in V I Miller, 'K voprosy o srvanitel'noi chislennosti partii Bol'shevikov i Men'shevikov v 1917 g', *Voprosy istorii KPSS* (1988), part 12 pp109-118. See also L Lande, 'Some Statistics of the Unification Congress, August 1917', in L Haimson (ed), op cit, pp389-391.
135   L Lande, op cit, pp4-5; B Sapir, op cit, p374.
136   L Lande, op cit, p43.
137   Quoted in B D Gal'perina, 'The Petrograd Soviet in September and October of 1917 (New Data)', *Voprosy Istorii* no 10 (1978), translated in *Studies in Soviet History*, vol xxiii, no 1, Summer 1984, pp89-90. This Soviet study contains some useful information to supplement more familiar Western accounts.
138   Z Galili, *Mensheviks...* op cit, p392, A Rabinowitch, *The Bolsheviks Come to Power: The Revolution of 1917 in Petrograd* (New York, 1976)
139   Malyantovich in S Jones, op cit.
140   Z Galili, *Liberals in the Russian Revolution*, op cit, p394.
141   R G Suny 'Revision and Retreat in the Historiography of 1917: Social History and its Critics', op cit. p167; C Read, op cit, pp148, 158 (my emphasis).
142   I have benefited enormously from an excellent critique of the social history school: J E Marot, 'Class Conflict, Political Competition and Social Transformation: Critical Perspectives on the Social History of the Russian Revolution', *Revolutionary Russia*, December 1994, vol 7, no2.
143   N Bukharin, op cit, p128.
144   G Swain, op cit, pp48-53. It should be made clear that when Swain speaks here of 'seizing power' he means political power. The question of economic and social power is resolutely ignored in the central part of his discussion.
145   G Swain, op cit, p57; L Lande, op cit, pp64 onwards.
146   Quoted T Cliff, *Trotsky: The Sword of the Revolution, 1917-1923* (Bookmarks, 1985), p25.
147   V D Nabokov, op cit.
148   Quoted J P Nettl, *Rosa Luxemburg* (Oxford University Press, 1969), p423, 425.

Prelude to revolution: class consciousness and the First World War

MEGAN TRUDELL

Over 80 years after it began the First World War continues to haunt our imaginations. The images of the trenches, the mud, the suffering, are ingrained onto our consciousness, whatever age we are. A drive through Northern France today means roads lined with cemeteries and monuments to the dead. Farmers still turn up tin hats and shells from the ground with every year's plough. The experience of war produced some of the 20th century's most provoking art in the work of Chagall, Otto Dix, Kathë Kollwitz and the German Expressionists, among others, and some of the most moving prose and poetry in the work of Graves, Owen, Sassoon, D H Lawrence, Blunden, Remarque and others. And the war continues to fascinate: some of the best selling books over the last few years—like Sebastian Faulks' *Birdsong* and Pat Barker's powerful *Regeneration* trilogy—have focused on the war, those who fought it, and those they left behind.

The reason the First World War intrigues is in part because it is not as easily explained as the Second World War. Whatever the truth of it, the Second World War is widely perceived as having a purpose: as a war against fascism. The First World War has no such justification. The puzzle remains—how to explain such a meaningless waste of human life.

And in part it remains the most shocking of wars, despite all the bloodshed humanity has seen since, because it was the first war fought with 20th century technology—a modern industrial war. One of the most horrific aspects of the war is the contradiction between generals intent on using 19th century methods like cavalry and bayonets in a situation of entrenched warfare and machine guns. It staggers the imagination that such idiocy held sway for so long, losing millions of lives, barely gaining any territory.

The war also had an enormous impact on the shape of the world. As one book puts it, 'The 1914-1918 conflict created the fundamental elements of 20th century history'.[1] When war broke out in August 1914 central Europe, Turkey and Russia were dominated by three powerful empires—the Tsars in Russia, the Austro-Hungarian, and the Ottoman. When it ended four years later, all three were in ruins, broken into a myriad nation states. The redistribution of power by the victorious Allies at Versailles established faultlines that still destabilise the late 20th century world. War in the Balkans and continual tension and conflict in the Middle East can be seen as the 'chickens of Versailles coming home to roost'.[2] Other aspects of 20th century history that we take for granted—the rise of the United States as the powerful world economy, the decline of Britain as a world power, the fight for the survival of the first workers' state in Russia and its subsequent destruction—are all consequences of the First World War and its aftermath. So too is the Second World War, just 22 years later, a result of the continuing arms race and growing militarism. The 'war to end all wars' did the very opposite.

But what is the most crucial element about the First World War for socialists is after a period of seeming despair for working class unity it raised the curtain on a revolutionary era that brought the world working class closer to emancipation than any other. It gave birth to an enormous revolutionary wave across the defeated nations, triggered by the Russian Revolution of 1917. Among the victors, Britain, France and Italy all saw social upheavals of varying intensity. As a prelude to world revolution the war and its effects are central.

The war

The war encompassed much of the world. It was fought on the Allied side by the British, French, Russians, and, from 1915, the Italians—plus Belgians, Serbians, Portuguese, Greeks, Romanians, Montenegrans, Japanese, Canadians, Australians, New Zealanders, and, from the end of 1917, the United States. The Central Powers were Germany, Austria-Hungary, Bulgaria and Turkey. Most of the fighting took place on the Western Front, a line about 475 miles long stretching from Belgium to Switzerland. After the opening phase of the war—four months of rapid movement which saw the German army sweep through Belgium, down through France and halt within 25 miles of Paris—the Allies pushed the Central Powers back at the Battle of the Marne to a line which stayed more or less static for the next four years. But the war was also fought out on the

Eastern Front in Poland and Russia; in Italy, Palestine, Syria, Mesopotamia (now Iraq), Persia (Iran), Turkey, Greece, Romania, and North Africa.

The total financial cost of the war has been estimated as equal to the combined 1914 wealth of Britain, Australia and New Zealand.[3] Marc Ferro has calculated the economic loss to France: 700,000 houses and 20,000 factories destroyed; 50,000 kilometres of roads and railways rendered unusable; 3 million hectares of land ruined; cereal production down by 40 percent; industrial production by 50 percent.[4]

The human cost was enormous. Those who fought on every side paid a heavy price. About 10 million people were killed or died as a result of the war. Germany lost 1.8 million, Russia 1.7 million, France 1.38 million, Austria-Hungary 1.29 million, Britain 743,000 and Italy 615,000. 'On average [there] was more than 5,600 soldiers killed on each day of the war'.[5] The French lost almost 20 percent of their men of fighting age, the Germans, 13 percent. 'The British lost a generation—half a million men under the age of 30'.[6]

The First World War involved the most extensive use of trench warfare: the hideous spectacle of men digging themselves into the ground—often their own graves—separated from the enemy by 'no man's land', a 'chaos of waterlogged shell-craters, ruined tree stumps, mud and abandoned corpses'[7] maybe 100 yards wide. Periodically they were launched at the enemy in what were effectively suicide missions. The big battles on the Western Front—the Marne, Verdun, the Somme, Passchendaele—saw an unprecedented butchery. France lost over 140,000 men in five days in August 1914—a product of 'the theory of the offensive' which meant the French generals threw men at German artillery without 'thought to surprise or concealment', their officers 'carrying swords held by hands sporting white gloves'.[8]

At Verdun, the war's longest battle, in five months an average of 100 shells a minute were fired—23 million in total. Two million men fought at Verdun, by the end of the battle half of them had been slaughtered. Out of 330 infantry battalions in the French army, 259 went through Verdun at some point—not to be relieved until part of their number were destroyed. 'Yet at the end of the encounter, the battle lines were about where they had been at the beginning'.[9] On the Somme, in the four months from 1 July 1916 over 1 million men died. The British dead stood at 95,675—20,000 of whom fell on the first day of the battle. The French lost 50,729, the Germans, 164,055. Over 60 percent of the Australian troops who fought in it were killed. German machine gunners watched in amazement as the British walked towards them, their officers in the front—a tactic the British ruling class moved away from as a quarter of Oxbridge graduates under 25 in the army in 1914 were killed—and were mown down.[10] When the battle ended in November, 'the British line had moved forward six miles, but was still three miles short of Bapaume, the first day's objective'.[11]

Passchendaele, the third battle of Ypres, symbolises the futility of trench warfare. Fought between July and November 1917, the wettest summer and autumn in memory turned the battlefield into a swamp. Men, animals and equipment were swallowed into the mud. The dead became stepping stones for the living. The continuation of the battle was simple slaughter. Away from the Western Front, the disastrous campaign at Gallipoli cost thousands of lives—most of them from the Commonwealth; the Eastern Front killed a higher proportion of those who fought than the Western Front, though not as murderous in total. Two million Russians, 10 percent of those mobilised, died, 'churned into gruel until casualties in the firing line should make rifles available'.[12]

In addition to the death toll of those who fought can be added the 62,000 US soldiers who died of flu, the 82,000 civilians in Serbia (compared to 45,000 soldiers) killed, the 1.5 million Armenians massacred between 1914 and 1919—a genocide flowing from the bloody fight to forge a nation out of the old Ottoman empire among Turkish and Kurdish speakers—and the estimated 750,000 German civilians who died as a result of the Allied blockade. From 1914 to 1922 between 4 and 5 million people became refugees.[13]

The First World War was the worst devastation the world had seen up to that point. It was the first major war involving all of Europe since 1815. It involved the mass of the populations of those countries which fought it:

> In most combatant countries, roughly 50 percent of the male population between the ages of 18 and 49 were in uniform...[in France and Germany] about 80 percent of men of military age were conscripted. Austria-Hungary mobilised 75 percent of its adult male population; Britain, Serbia and Turkey called up between 50 and 60 percent. In Russia about 16 million men...served during the war.[14]

Hundreds of thousands of others worked in munitions, in mines, in rail—all economic life bent before the war. Such a massive upheaval arose not, as we are taught, from the petty incident that was used as its justification—the shooting of the Archduke Ferdinand in Sarajevo—or because of some personality flaws among the protagonists. It is quite possible that the Kaiser was bitter because of his shrivelled arm, but the notion that war was somehow a result of his 'volatility of mood and mind'[15] will not do as an explanation for mass butchery. The motivating force behind the eventual clash between the world's key nations was the increasing need of sections of capital to expand production beyond domestic borders and acquire new markets for goods. The enormous industrial growth of the late 19th and early 20th centuries had led to the increasing internationalisation of capitalism. Britain's star was fading, new powerful economies were jostling for room to expand. Germany and the United States began eating into Britain's domestic market. 'A number of competing national industrial economies now confronted each other. Under these circumstances economic competition became inextricably woven into the political, even the military, actions of states'.[16] That competition led to 'national rivalry for world markets and material resources', competition for control of oil rich areas, and to the potential for *unlimited* expansion for big companies.[17]

The war was the result of the antagonism between states locked in competition for the world's resources. Each state had its own specific motivation for war—whether it was the expansion of its resources, or protection of the empire it already held:

> *British and French capitalism, though weaker economically* [than Germany], *had much more powerful global presences... Sections of German capital wanted to expand outwards beyond their national boundaries in a similar way. The British and French ruling classes sought to protect their holdings by an alliance with Tsarist Russia against Germany and its allies, Austria-Hungary and the decaying Turkish empire. Rival imperialisms pushed against each other's influence in Morocco, in East and Southern Africa, above all in South East Europe.*[18]

The fact that the war was fought between nations that were growing in economic strength and industrial capabilities, coupled with the unlimited spoils which would fall to the victors meant that it was massively bloody— a mass produced war. Since 'the main participants were powerful industrial societies, each had to mobilise its full potential. The war became one of attrition in which victory could not be gained until one's enemy had been bled dry'.[19] And the war itself fed into the increasing industrial might of nations. Arms production accelerated economic growth—the French munitions industry maintained an output of 200,000 shells a day, Tsarist Russia produced 150,000. 'Mass war required mass production'.[20]

Nationalism

Such a cataclysm was bound to create social shock waves that would rock the world's ruling classes. But it certainly did not appear at the start that revolutions would be a result of the conflict. The strength of nationalist feeling in the first year of the war is an aspect of the war that perplexes many—why was the patriotic frenzy so great and why did so many workers volunteer to fight so enthusiastically? The notion that nationalism is all powerful is often used to bolster the argument that all the ruling class has to do is wave the flag and workers will flock behind it. It is an argument not restricted to the First World War but one encountered during every subsequent war—right up to the modern examples of the Falklands, the Gulf and Bosnia. The question of whether or not nationalism is a more powerful impulse than class identification is therefore utterly bound up with any account of the war.

The growth of nationalist sentiment was an inevitable corollary of the push to imperialism on the part of the great powers. The acquisition of territory and markets were justified as being in the 'national interest'. In the second half of the 19th century,

> the dynastic empires which had previously been the most bitter opponents of national movements began to redefine themselves in nationalist terms. The Prussian monarchy took over the German nationalist ideology. The Habsburg monarchy split its domains into two halves, in one of which Hungarian replaced Latin as the official language, in the other, German. The 'Tsar of all the Russias'... for the first time began to encourage a Great Russian nationalism.

The same period also saw the growth of the national idea in the more established capitalist states, where, for example, a 'new celebration of British nationalism, with the establishment, for the first time, of a state run educational system that indoctrinated children in the glories of "national" history, the writing of nationalist popular novels, plays, poetry and songs by literary admirers of the empire and the conscious invention of traditions aimed at encouraging popular identification with the monarchy'.[21]

In addition, the development of nationalism by the ruling classes meant the assertion of a dominant nationalism and thus the oppression of other national groups. But in this respect the stress on the national idea was double edged. As the imperialist war loomed many national minorities began to find their voices. This was especially true in Russia, where 57 percent of the population were national minorities, and in the Austro-Hungarian empire, which was built on the denial of national rights to many of its national groups. As a result national movements grew, especially among the Southern Slavs, threatening the dynasty's very existence.[22]

To trace the mass acceptance of nationalism during the beginning of the war, it is necessary to look at the state of the class struggle immediately before the war. What is frequently overlooked is the fact that the war was preceded not only by a rise in nationalist feeling but also by a wave of revolutionary upheaval and strikes—there had been revolutions in 1905 in Russia, following the end of the Russo-Japanese War, in Turkey in 1907 and in Mexico in 1912. These 'added new combustible material to a world already preparing to go up in flames'.[23]

In Russia before the war there was a serious heightening of class tensions—just days before the war broke out there were barricades erected in St Petersburg and a strike of 200,000 in protest at police brutality against a demonstration by workers from the Putilov factory held in solidarity with striking oil workers. In Britain, the Great Unrest of 1910-1914 saw a huge upsurge of militant unofficial strikes that swept mining, transport and engineering. The British ruling class was deeply shaken by the biggest workers' movement since the Chartists. Trotsky wrote, 'The vague shadow of revolution hovered over Britain in those days'.[24] Germany saw a wave of strikes in favour of widening the franchise between 1910-1912, often involving clashes with the police. The years 1911-1914 were also years of crisis in Italian society: there was a general strike called in response to the conquest of Libya, and in the years just before the war there were big struggles, particularly in Turin and Milan.

The outbreak of the war broke the back of the revolts. Patriotism swept every country involved. It seemed to some to be 'an outbreak of unreason, madness, or a mass delusion'.[25] The popular conception of the declaration of war, with cheering crowds waving off trainloads of excited soldiers is not unfounded—many workers in France and Britain, Germany, Austro-Hungary and Russia volunteered enthusiastically to fight. In France, the expected level of desertion was 5-13 percent, in reality only 1.5 percent refused to fight.[26] In Britain '750,000 volunteered in the first 8 weeks, a further million in the next 8 months'.[27] In Russia 1 million deserters were expected. All but a few thousand, out of 15 million, failed to go. From a near revolutionary situation to enthusiasm for war—'Russia seemed to have been completely transformed', wrote the British ambassador of the time.[28]

In part this enthusiasm was a response to ruling class propaganda about the nature of the war. Every ruling class involved argued the war was one of national defence. Germany was defending itself from Russian aggression, France from German militarism. Britain was defending 'poor little Belgium'. Each ruling class pushed the idea that there was an outside threat to the democratic rights enjoyed by the nation's citizens, and in part the response of each country's working class was an identification with one's nation and a desire to protect one's way of life.

But it wasn't a straightforward calculation on the part of the ruling classes involved. Such had been the scale of domestic crisis in most of the countries involved that it was not at all obvious that workers would respond to the call to arms. In Britain, against a background of social upheaval and a potentially explosive situation in Ireland where the pressure for Home Rule was mounting, the Liberal minister John Morley considered that 'the atmosphere of war cannot be friendly to order in a

democratic system that is verging on the humour of [18]48'.[29] Ruling
classes across the globe were in fact astonished by the scale of patriotic
zeal. This should not be surprising: nationalism is not simply imposed
from above, but has to in some way correspond to existing national sentiments among a section at least of the population—often the middle
class—and grips the minds of the masses when other social change
seems remote.

It is not simply the case that workers who had fought so hard for social
change in the pre-war years suddenly turned their backs on their own
struggles and were brainwashed by their respective governments. Much
of their motivation can be traced precisely to the holding back, or even
defeat, of such social struggles. The vision of war came to seem as if it
were an alternative way of dramatically transforming society. Magnus
Hirschfeld described the response to the declaration of war as 'a discharge
of tensions that had built up for years'.[30] Ferro argues that the 'worker of
1914, going off to war, had found a substitute for revolutionary hopes.'
Many workers went to fight with 'an image of war as the antithesis of the
boredom, materiality and mechanisation of every day life'.[31] Trotsky,
living in Vienna when war broke out, described the jubilation in the
streets and pointed to the fact that, for millions, the war represented a
moment of profound change:

> *The people whose lives, day in and day out, pass in a monotony of hopeless-*
> *ness are many; they are the mainstay of modern society. The alarm of*
> *mobilisation breaks into their lives like a promise; the familiar and long-hated*
> *is overthrown, and the new and unusual reigns in its place. Changes still more*
> *incredible are in store for them in the future. For better or worse? For the*
> *better, of course—what can seem worse...than 'normal' conditions?*[32]

It is important to grasp how dramatic a period people felt they were
entering. There was a real sense that the whole shape of the world was
about to change and that society was embarking on an adventure.
Gertrude Bäumer, writing in Germany, has summed this feeling up:

> *The plunge from out of the existing world into a completely different one*
> *cannot be described... There are no expressions suitable to the reality of this*
> *pause between two world orders—the fading of everything that was important*
> *yesterday and the summoning up of novel historical forces. In those clear*
> *sleepless nights of high summer we became a 'battleground of two epochs'.*[33]

In the beginning, that feeling for change connected with the patriotism and the celebration of the national idea pushed from the ruling class
and echoed by labour leaders. But nationalist enthusiasm, though by far

the most powerful impulse at the start of the war, was by no means the only response to the hostilities. There were huge demonstrations against the war and mass rallies for peace in France, in Britain and in Germany just days before the war broke out—a movement that was, days later, reined in by socialist party and trade union leaders.

Nationalism and revolutionary ideas are, logically, mutually exclusive—but the gap between workers' interests and their perception of those interests means that they often hold conflicting ideas, like defending their nation and wanting social justice at the same time. Which outweighs the other depends on social circumstances, individual experience, the level of class struggle and so on. Rosa Luxemburg, the Polish-German revolutionary, described at the start of the war the potential for change in people's ideas:

> *The psyche of the masses like the eternal sea always carries all the latent possibilities: the deathly calm and the roaring storm, the lowest cowardice and the wildest heroism. The mass is always that which it **must** be according to the circumstances of the time, and the mass is always at the point of becoming something entirely different than what it appears to be.*[34]

Future Communist Party leader Harry Pollitt, working during the war as a boilermaker in Britain, looked concretely at the same process: 'It was my experience time and time again that the workers you mixed with every day, who respected you, who listened to your arguments and suggestions, who you never thought could be swept off their feet by jingoism...could by one incident or another be so transformed, though perhaps only temporarily, that they did not appear to be the same people'.[35]

The First World War, rather than simply demonstrating the strength of nationalism over social or class consciousness, actually provides a stark example of how the balance between the two (and many other ideas) constantly shifts.

The war changed people, especially those who fought in it. A 'deep and profound alteration of identity' took place.[36] Many previously held ideas were thrown into chaos and abandoned, reworked or subsumed by other, new ways of looking at the world. Class conflicts did not disappear, despite the hopes of some, mainly middle class officers, that the war would present some sort of 'natural community'. Every army was vulnerable to the 'realities of a war that expressed, even amplified the class hatreds endemic to bourgeois society'.[37] And the more the idea of the war as a classless enterprise was insisted on by the elite, the bitterer the disappointments when soldiers faced the reality of army hierarchy, bullying by often savage officers, and all the humiliations of being oppressed and exploited.

One officer in the German army wrote of the differences between volunteer soldiers and conscripts that 'they felt towards us a kind of class hostility, or at least a class barrier'.[38] Karl Jannack, the son of a railway worker and an SPD member in Bremen before the war described the differences:

> There were two different groups of reserve people: replacements for men and officer candidates. Of the first there is little to say…they disappeared into the trenches like ourselves. The others were almost all volunteers, mostly graduates of secondary school and sons of wealthy tradesmen, high officials, or senators. With them came their fathers with their automobiles, their cars were always packed full with parcels.[39]

Franz Schauwecker, the son of a customs official in Hamburg, was one of those idealistic young officers who went to the front imagining a community of honour and discovered that he was the target of class hatred: 'Inside my company my own comrades—for the most part dock workers from Stettin—played tricks on me with genuine rapture whenever possible, even after the first big battle, because they, the men of action, saw in me the…foolish war volunteer…and because they, the socialist workers, saw in me the pampered, well-to-do, privileged man of education'.[40] As E J Leed says, 'The organic dependence of a male community, the cessation of individuality, the submergence of class differences—all of his expectations—cast no shadow in the glare of realities'.[41]

In the 1920s and 1930s, Schauwecker evidently swept the memory of this class conflict from his mind, becoming an ardent nationalist who romanticised the war as a 'national experience'. He wrote: 'In 1914 the German people marched forth, in November 1918 the German nation returned. In between lay the breakthrough of nationalism into the political reality as being and fact'.[42] It is no accident that, in those who looked to the national ideal after the war, the middle class officer was well represented. The nation state was often an aspiration most fervently held by the middle class, and their imaginings of what the war would be like fitted with the ideal of a national whole. The fact of war itself only served to reinforce this sentiment in some: 'It has been hammered into us with blood and dirt and sweat for four years; we are not for ourselves alone. We are a complete, closed body, a nation'.[43] Leed argues that although the war was a deeply disillusioning experience, especially for the sons of the bourgeoisie, nevertheless, those with the highest expectations of the glories of war were among the later popularisers of nationalist doctrine. But it was not a nationalism born *during* war, if anything the experience of war *weakened* nationalism. It was an ideal resurrected after the fact.

The strong sense of the national idea was initially overwhelming for millions of workers as well. They did pick up weapons against workers from other countries and fight each other for four years. Yet, even at first, there were small signs that it would prove a weaker bond than it was for the middle and upper classes. The experiences of truces between enemy soldiers that occurred throughout the war, the hatred for officers amongst men, were contradictory sentiments which pulled in the opposite direction to the notion of fighting together, all classes, for one nation against another. An often repeated example of the slender hold of nationalism in the face of shared experience and army hierarchies—even in the middle of war—are the events of Christmas 1914. On Christmas Eve along some parts of the German line on the Western Front the soldiers put Christmas trees on the trench parapets. The 'enemy' troops sang hymns and applauded each others' efforts. Rifleman Graham Williams remembered:

> *First the Germans would sing one of their carols and then we would sing one of ours, until when we started up 'O Come All Ye Faithful' the Germans immediately joined in singing the same hymn to the Latin words 'Adeste Fideles'. And I thought, well, this was really a most extraordinary thing—two nations both singing the same carol in the middle of a war.*[44]

And Christmas 1914 is simply one of the better known examples of fraternisation that became commonplace. Even at the front under strict discipline officers could not prevent unofficial, totally illegal truces between men. One soldier described how it worked:

> *In a quiet position everything is done to maintain, if at all possible, the calm. If one knocks out the opponents' bunkers...the other does the same, and both lay exposed under the open sky and no one has won anything...for this reason orders for patrols to take prisoners find little approval and few volunteers.*[45]

Resentment against the high command was often 'translated into subtle, collective action, which thwarted the high command trench war strategy'.[46] British or French soldiers out on patrol would pass by a German patrol without a shot being fired, it was common to fly a white flag at a certain point on the trench parapet beyond which was the toilet, and the 'enemy' would not fire on that area. Men were only prevented from exchanging cigarettes or postcards across no man's land by official crackdowns. In other words, social inclinations often cut across and intersected with feelings of national identification and, the longer the stalemate on the Western Front continued, the more soldiers' resentment was aimed at their own commanders.

Less than a year after the war started, class consciousness began to reassert itself. The economic side effects of war were a key contributory factor to this resistance. The strikes that broke out in most countries after the first year of war were motivated largely by the huge disparity between the wage cuts, freezes and sacrifices expected from workers on the one hand and the enormous profits bosses were making off the back of mass slaughter. Prices for food and clothing rose massively across the board—by 80 percent in Italy, 70 percent in Britain, 600 percent in Germany. Industries like oil, chemicals, metals and leathers, which had been declining or making a loss before 1914, boomed. In Germany declared profits rose by 10 million marks in six months in 1917. In Britain and America, the profits of new industries like Anglo-Persian oil rose from a deficit of £26,700 in 1914 to profits of £85,000 in 1916, £344,100 in 1917 and more than £1 million in 1918. Profits of rubber companies rose 40 times in the four years of war. In the US, Washington Iron and Steel saw profits more than double from £184 million to £485 million and Anaconda Copper's profits went up from £9 million to £51 million between 1916 and 1917 alone.

But the gap between the profits of the rich and the privations of the masses meant that strikes in Russia, Germany, Britain and France increased dramatically between 1915 and 1917. In Italy, although the number of strikes was lower, the number of workers on strike rose.[47] September 1915 in Russia was pictured in one report like this:

> *The workers, and the population as a whole, are gripped by some sort of madness and are like gunpowder...I must also note the presence, in Moscow, of about 30,000 convalescent soldiers. This is a wild band, not recognising discipline, making scandals, clashing with the police (recently one of the latter was killed by soldiers), freeing prisoners and so on. Undoubtedly, if there are disorders, this whole horde will be on the side of the crowd.*[48]

In November of the same year: 'Sailors...began to clamour for better food, more humane treatment,' as well as the 'dismissal of all officers bearing German names'.[49]

In Germany, class collaboration was taken to its highest extreme with the vast majority of the representatives of the working class supporting actively imperialist policies. Unions 'became agents of the state, denouncing "agitators" hostile to the agreements concluded with ruling classes and governments'.[50] Yet there were growing demonstrations for peace from 1915 on. These began numbering only hundreds in Berlin, but escalated as hunger drove people into the streets. When Karl Liebnecht, the revolutionary and the first Reichstag deputy to vote against war credits, was arrested on a May Day demonstration in 1916, 55,000 workers struck in solidarity during his trial.[51] Feeling against the war grew: by December 1915 there were 20 Reichstag deputies voting against war credits. The food situation in Germany deteriorated. In 1916 the bread ration dropped and the potato crop failed, leading to the terrible 'turnip winter' of 1916-1917. As real wages fell rapidly, the demand for peace became widespread among the masses in German society, while the Allied blockade pushed the German military establishment to continue the war—thus polarising German society.

In Britain workers in 15 percent of industry struck on 8 August 1914, just after the Defence of the Realm Act was passed. By 1915 there was increasing resistance to bosses holding down wages and putting up prices. In the south Wales coalfields and on the Clyde, government intransigence and repression led to strikes which spilled over into conflict with the state. The formation of the Clyde Workers Committee promoted shop stewards' committees in each workshop. Its chief militants were deported from Clydeside, but they spread the practice to other cities, notably Sheffield. In November 1916, after the casualties of the Somme had devastated so many British families, the call up of an exempted engineer from Sheffield provoked a 10,000 strong strike. Flying pickets were sent to other workplaces to spread the strike. The War Office backed down and the dispute led to permanent shop stewards' committees in Sheffield. Back on the Clyde there were attempts to link the economic strikes with a fight against the war. John Maclean courageously spoke out against the war and stood out as an internationalist in a sea of opportunism but he faced an uphill struggle: 'Maclean's ideas were not backed up by any solid organisation so had only minimal influence on the rank and file…[he] had no mechanism (such as a party rooted in the factories) to fight for internationalism'.[52] Having to work within the shop stewards' committee put obvious constraints on Maclean's ability to build widespread opposition to the war among the masses—the committee was not a revolutionary party and could not be won to putting anti-war politics at the centre of its platform.

In Italy the war led to repressive measures against those attempting to leave a job and those advocating pacifism. The Socialist Party (PSI) was against the war but did little to organise real resistance to imperialism. The war was squeezing the economy hard, railways were only running to 50 percent capacity, textile factories' production was half the pre-war figure, agricultural production was hit—leading to bread shortages. Strikes broke out over wages and on May Day 1917 there were large anti-war demonstrations. These demonstrations grew in size, reaching their peak in the summer in Turin where 'the strikes…were reminiscent in many ways of those in Petrograd in February. Women and youth had a vital part in them, trying to fraternise with the *carabinieri* and shouting, "Don't fire at your brothers"'.[53]

Though strike figures for France were lower than those in Britain or Italy, they nonetheless increased, despite the bombing of Paris and the continued presence on French soil of Central Powers troops. According to Ferro they were 'not purely economic in motive, but were stimulated by a climate of political agitation and militancy'.[54]

In part all this was due also to the changing composition of the working classes in warring countries: the sheer numbers of men who left to fight meant an influx of women and younger men into the factories—in France nearly a quarter of those employed in the defence industries were women; in Germany the number of women workers rose from 1.4 million to 2.1 million during the war. In the US the number of women workers increased by two and a half times. In Germany the number of miners under the age of 16 rose by seven times and the number of similarly aged metal workers rose by four times. The same pattern was evident in Britain and Russia.[55] The newer workers, without the experiences of struggles that had been defused in the pre-war years, were often more militant.

The reality therefore was very far from the national community: 'The actuality of war raised with new intensity and concreteness the problems that had been "solved" with its declaration: the relationship between social classes, the relationship of men to the means of production that in war became the means of destruction, the relationship between owners, "managers", and workers of war'.[56] Trotsky described the process:

> Like revolution, war forces life, from top to bottom, away from the beaten track. But revolution directs its blows against the established power. War, on the contrary, at first strengthens the state power which, in the chaos engendered by war, appears to be the only firm support—and then undermines it.[57]

Historian Eric Hobsbawm, in his book *Nations and Nationalism*, cites a study which looks at a large number of letters from soldiers writing home to Austria-Hungary. The war and the impact of the Russian Revolution filtered through to every level of society, raising new political ideas:

> Among the activists of some of the oppressed nationalities such as the Poles and Ukrainians, the event raised hopes of reform—perhaps even of independence. However, the dominant mood was a desire for peace and **social** transformation... Even where we find the strongest national tone—as among the Czech, Serbian and Italian letters—we also find an overwhelming wish for social transformation.[58]

Nationalism and class consciousness existed together and conflicted in workers' heads. As Hobsbawm puts it:

Men and women did not choose collective identification as they chose shoes, knowing that one could only put on one pair at a time. They had, and still have, several attachments and loyalties simultaneously, including nationality, and are simultaneously concerned with various aspects of life, any of which may at any one time be foremost in their minds, as occasion suggests. For long periods of time these different attachments would not make incompatible demands on a person...it was only when one of these loyalties conflicted directly with another or others that a problem of choosing between them arose...supporting their own government in war seemed to ordinary workers quite compatible with demonstrating class consciousness and hostility to employers. The south Wales miners who shocked their revolutionary syndicalist, and internationalist, leaders by rushing to the colours equally readily brought the coalfield out on general strike less than a year later, deaf to the accusation that they were unpatriotic.[59]

Understanding the strength of the national idea this way cuts through the notion that war *proves* that nationalism will always triumph over working class unity. A massive shift took place in the heads of millions of workers and soldiers between 1914 and 1917. Once people are swung by patriotism, or won over by nationalism, it does not follow that they are *wholly* captured by chauvinism or that they cannot swing away from it. The contrast between the patriotic fervour of the first year of the war and the revolutions, in part against the war, that ultimately ended it ought to be proof that national feeling does not preclude dawning class consciousness or desire for wider change. As Hobsbawm says:

Progress of national consciousness...is neither linear nor necessarily at the expense of other elements of social consciousness. Seen from the perspective of August 1914, one might have concluded that nation and nation-state had triumphed over all rival social and political loyalties. Could one have said so in the perspective of 1917?[60]

By 1918, 'Patriotic sentiment no longer absorbed, as in 1914, the social struggle. The war had come as a revelation, a detonator that blew up one element of the old system of authority'.[61]

But if the war polarised society, it did not simply engender revolution. Ex-soldiers were not uniformly revolutionary—the *Croix de Feu*, a far right veterans' organisation, fought the workers' movement in France in 1936. Hitler was a young soldier in the war. People who lost faith in the war, or became weary with the sheer numbers of dead, experienced conflicting emotions: confusion and fear as well as anger. It is not a surprise that some retreated into suspicion of the foreign, and blind clinging to jingoism. In some cases—Germany, Austria, Hungary, Italy—nationalism 're-emerged not as a milder substitute for social revolution, but as the mobilisation of ex-officers, lower middle and middle class civilians for counter-revolution. It emerged as the matrix of fascism'.[62]

Otto Braun, a German junior officer killed in 1918, understood that the shift in many soldiers' consciousness was not a clear cut thing, not necessarily fully thought through, at least at first:

> *Any leaning the soldier may have towards socialism is...mainly negative. He is furious with the whole rotten bourgeois society, furious with the stay-at-homes, in fact furious with everything at home... [When the soldiers return]...there will be a great amount of knowledge and a consciousness of power in back of them. In order to guide these masses into the paths of productive activity, one will have to know and be able to direct their gigantic mass of uncontrolled energy.*[63]

It is doubtful that the productive activity Braun had in mind was the revolution, but his words applied to those who would win soldiers to socialism.

Acceptance by workers of society's ruling ideas can and does change. In the sort of social turmoil that the war brought to all the major powers new ideas of peace and social change conflicted with old allegiances and heightened nationalist sentiment. For a while, perhaps a long while, depending on the outside circumstances, workers can carry ideas that do not seem compatible with each other. In the long term, one or the other will come to the fore, but which depends on individual experience, the level of social conflict, and the poles of attraction and options available.

Reformism

The role of reformists was key to securing working class support for the war. The support of the leaders of the Second International—the collective voice of the world's socialist parties representing 3 million workers in 27 different parties—for their own governments in the war led many millions of workers into the slaughter of the trenches. But it didn't start that way. On 25 July 1914 the executive of the German Social Democratic Party (SPD) issued an appeal to its membership to demonstrate against the impending war:

> *In the name of humanity and of civilisation the class conscious proletariat of Germany protests fervently against these criminal machinations of the warmongers... Not a drop of German soldiers' blood must be sacrificed to the lust for power of the Austrian rulers, and in the interests of imperialist profits... Our*

cry must ring in the ears of the rulers everywhere: We want no war! Down with
the war! Long live the international brotherhood of the peoples![64]

On 4 August, however, every SPD deputy obeyed the majority decision to vote for the war credits the government wanted. At one stroke the
most powerful socialist party in the world at the time capitulated to its
own ruling class and to nationalism. Its tortuous justification was that the
war was a defensive war:

We are carrying out what we have pledged ourselves to do: we do not desert
the fatherland in its hour of peril. In this respect we are in complete accord
with the International which has always recognised the right of every nation
to independence and self-defence... We trust that the hard experience of war
will awaken in millions of people a horror of war, and will win them over for
the ideals of socialism and of peace on earth. Guided by these principles we
shall vote for the requisite credits.[65]

The betrayal, shocking though it was, was the result of contradictions
that had long plagued the International. The 1890s, formative years for
the SPD, had seen increasing prosperity and stability in Germany. Trade
unions became legalised and grew and the SPD became less oriented on
struggle and more committed to gaining parliamentary influence. This
material stability was given ideological expression by Edward Bernstein
who argued in 1898 for a revision of Marxism. The need for revolution
had passed, and the SPD should present itself as it really was—a
reformist social democratic party. Although initially resisted by both the
centrist current in the SPD and the left led by Rosa Luxemburg, the aftermath of the 1905 Russian revolution led to a break between the centre
and the left. The centrist position, outlined by Karl Kautsky, now became
one which saw the class struggle as a 'strategy of attrition', rather than
one of insurrection. Increasingly revisionism was tolerated by the centre
and, in the elections of 1912, the SPD's emergence as the largest party in
Germany seemed to confirm the wisdom of the electoral strategy. Steady
integration into the German establishment meant that the national identity of the SPD clashed with its slogans of internationalism. These
cracks, papered over in the years before the war, were revealed as deep
chasms on 4 August 1914.

Taking their cue from the SPD, trade union leaders suspended strikes
and established a policy of class collaboration, known as the *Burgfrieden*
in Germany and the *union sacrée* in France. The party and trade union
leaders bent themselves to 'the identification of the working class with
the destiny of the nation',[66] unwilling to lose support from the working
class, or from the government, they did not argue against the war. The
pressure to support the ruling class for the SPD, and the extent to which

its leading members had already travelled down the reformist road, was well illustrated by a member from the left of the party, Konrad Haenisch:

> *The conflict of two souls in one breast was probably easy for none of us...*[On the one hand] *this driving, burning desire to throw oneself into the powerful current of the general national tide, and, on the other, the terrible spiritual fear of following that desire fully, of surrendering oneself to the mood which roared about one and which, if one looked deep into one's heart, had long since taken possession of the soul. This fear: will you not also betray yourself and your cause?... [Thus it was] until suddenly...the terrible tension was resolved...until—despite all principles and wooden theories—one could, for the first time in almost a quarter century, join with a full heart, a clean conscience and without a sense of treason in the sweeping, stormy song: 'Deutschland, Deutschland, Über Alles'.*[67]

In the name of socialism and world peace, the leaders of the socialist movement in Germany sent millions of young men to their deaths. They threw away the potential to oppose the war at the outset. The SPD's capitulation was the most stunning to the socialist movement but it was by no means a response isolated to Germany. During August, Belgium's Emile Vandervelde, the executive secretary of the Second International's leading bureau, entered his country's war cabinet. The editorial in the Belgian socialist daily, *Le Peuple*, stressed the need in the 'hour of final victory...without superfluous compassion...to cast out the teutonic race from the family of humanity'.[68] In France, the Socialist Party and its union, the CGT, organised mass rallies and protests up to the outbreak of war. On 25 July the CGT paper, *La Bataille Syndicaliste*, urged a 'revolutionary general strike' in the event of war breaking out. On 1 August, general mobilisation in France was proclaimed with the declaration of war on Russia by Germany. The response of *La Bataille Syndicaliste* was to tell workers, 'If you should be killed in action, all those of your comrades who as yet remain behind...swear solemnly, while bidding you farewell: vanguard soldiers of the revolution, you will not have died in vain'.[69]

The CGT general secretary, Jouhaux, at the funeral of Jean Jaures—the Socialist Party leader assassinated by a right winger—declared that 'it is not hatred of the German people, but of German imperialism which drives us onto the battlefield'. He claimed to speak 'in the name of the workers who have gone to war, who will go, of whom I am one'—although he did no such thing. The French Socialists also voted for war credits and, on 26 August, Guesde and Sembat, leading Socialists, entered the government. Guesde later, in January 1918 justified their actions, saying, 'Class collaboration in politics and government in peacetime is the worst kind of trickery, on the social level, because it preserves capitalist *society*, the destruction of which is essential for the freedom of labour and humanity as a whole; but in wartime, on the national level, it becomes just as much a duty for socialists, because it defends the nation, against aggressive war, and thus maintains the indispensable framework for socialist activity today and the first condition for internationalism tomorrow'.[70]

Marc Ferro sees the capitulation of the socialist leaders as inevitable in the face of all encompassing patriotism: 'For Frenchman and German alike, patriotism had defeated the International...men passionately welcomed the war and socialists seemed to be living in a world apart'.[71] And it is true that workers in every country were bombarded by a ruling class ideological offensive in support of the war. Many activists were thrown sideways by the national fervour and feared isolation from the masses. But, as we have seen, there was plenty of reason for the ruling class to be nervous of the response from its populations. The role of social democrat leaders in encouraging their members to defend their respective governments, in convincing those who looked to them that fighting an imperialist war was the 'duty of socialists', was crucial to the governments' ability to win over their workers. The fact that the leaders tried to justify their capitulation on the pragmatic grounds of not losing support in a war they initially believed would be short lived in no way lessened the disastrous impact of their actions on those they were meant to represent.

Trotsky wrote of Britain in the period just before the war, 'The leaders exerted all their strength in order to paralyse the movement...strengthening the bourgeoisie and thus preparing the way for the imperialist slaughter'.[72] By braking the struggle labour leaders ensured that the only way to prevent the war—through workers' resistance and the refusal to fight or build weapons of destruction—was blocked. Had the leaders of the Second International refused to back the war, and continued to encourage workers to respond to the call to slaughter with strike action against the employers, the possibility existed that significantly fewer of the 10 million people who lost their lives need have done so. The Second International was not beaten by patriotism—it never fought it. And in accepting the priorities of defence of the nation above internationalism it committed suicide. In the words of one French writer, 'The International died on 4 August, 1914, killed not by the war, but by the renunciation of the socialists themselves'.[73]

Did there need to be a war?

The leaders of the main social democratic parties justified their attitude to the war with an analysis of capitalism that sees it as a basically sound system in which the occasional diplomatic mistake leads to war. War is seen as an aberration, rather than an in-built consequence of the competition that is central to the system. Karl Kautsky, for instance, wrote that the growth of cartels meant agreement between different sections of capital and this was mirrored by co-operation between nations in developing new markets. He argued that this would, at least, postpone war for some time. War is, according to Kautsky, not the result of the competitive anarchy of capitalism, but an illogical move that ruling classes can avoid. This is a view held by many academics and historians today. A related argument is that there would have been no revolutionary upheaval without the war. On this view revolution is an abberation resting on another abberation, war. Thus revolution is twice removed from its origins in the essential nature of capitalism. Norman Stone, for example, in his book on the Eastern Front, sees the Russian Revolution as a direct result of the war: 'The First World War provoked a crisis of economic modernisation, and Bolshevik Revolution was the outcome'.[74]

That the war itself fed into and was a powerful motivating force in the revolutions that swept Europe between 1917 and 1923 is not in question. But the common view that without the First World War there would have been no such revolt is one with which Marxists should take issue—revolutions occur when society breaks down, it is true, but it was not necessary for 10 million people to die first.

The first point to remember is that the war broke the rising tide of struggle in the years after 1910. War does not emerge from stability, but from a system in crisis and flux—but the same is true of large scale social revolt. The period before the war was one of growing hostilities between great powers, born of increasing need for expansion of capital and the acquisition of territory and, therefore, markets. It was also one in which the upheaval in the system was producing opposition to imperialism, both from the socialist movement and in the beginnings of the ferment among oppressed nations. The world working class was growing, was more concentrated than ever before, and was increasingly militant in many countries. The fact that the jostling for influence among imperialist nations led to war and that crisis fed into revolution is not the same thing as a simple equation that war equals revolution. The Gulf War did not lead to revolution, nor have the numerous wars in Africa—it is not an inevitable outcome. There have also been revolutions without wars: Mexico before the First World War and the revolutions in Eastern Europe in 1989 are two examples. Wars and revolutions can come from the same basic source and pull people in very different directions. At the root of such upheaval is a fundamentally unstable system—with a vast number of 'aberrations' to its name as the 20th century draws to a close.

Subsequent events have proved Kautsky wrong, and shown that the crisis in society can either be resolved in favour of the system which perpetuates war or in favour of workers' revolutions which hold within them the seed of a society free from war. The period of the First World War and the first successful workers' revolution posed that choice starkly, and those who chose to defend the existing system turned their backs on the possibility of ending war for good.

February 1917

The rising level of protests and strikes against the war that were a feature of 1915 and 1916 exploded into decisive battle in Russia in February 1917. War weariness had provoked massive anger. A police report in early 1917 stated that the working class was,

> *on the edge of despair...the slightest explosion, however trivial its pretext, will lead to uncontrollable riots...The inability to buy goods, the frustrations of queuing, the rising death rate owing to poor living conditions, and the cold and damp produced by lack of coal...have all created a situation where most of the workers are ready to embark on the savage excesses of a food riot.*[75]

February also saw the introduction of rationing. Soldiers refused their officers' orders to fire on the rioters, instead marching with them to the Duma—the Tsarist parliament—shouting, 'Bread!', 'Down with the Tsar!', and 'Stop the war!' The Tsar was deposed, replaced by a Provisional government headed by a representative of the monarchy, Prince L'vov, and including the Socialist Revolutionary Kerensky. By 17 March workers in 49 towns had set up their own soviets, by 22 March another 28 had joined them. The soldiers also established their own revolutionary committees. A situation of dual power prevailed between the workers' and soldiers' democratic councils on the one hand and the official government on the other.

The war had initially cloaked the crisis in Russian society, numbing the revolts against the Tsar. The reality of war now fed into the crisis and exacerbated it. Conditions that arose as a direct result of the war provoked widespread bitterness and resistance. Almost more importantly, the political consequences of a revolt against a government in time of war was huge. It may take longer for workers to take the state on, clouded by nationalism and identification with their own ruling class, but when it becomes clear that the oppressed classes are bearing the burden of war alone it sharpens class conflict immeasurably. In addition, governments and the state are forced to tie themselves much more closely to capital—to defend and protect the ability to compete and profit—and that relationship is never clearer than at a time of great crisis like war. The connection in workers' heads, once made, creates politically combustible material. The bosses are no longer separate from government. The division between economic protests and political ones breaks down and the possibility of organising to attain both food and peace is placed on the agenda.

Even after the February Revolution, however, the war was not universally condemned. Some workers—in chemicals, artillery, engineering and rail especially—had been given wage rises as a result of increased profits. Although more than eaten up by price rises, these workers relied on the war for a living and were disproportionately affected by patriotism. For them, the new government meant democracy; Russia was now in line with the other Allied states, and the war could be prosecuted more successfully, not necessarily ended.

In the army, however, the threat to the continued prosecution of the war stemmed from the changes in discipline that the soldiers, flush with new found power, imposed on their officers. One general reported that, 'Each time I gave an order, the soldiers said, "No, you can't do that"'.[76] The contradictions inside the heads of Russia's soldiers are clear from the claims set out by the 15th rifle regiment: along with pay increases and improvement in medical conditions was a request that soldiers' families would be looked after so they could continue to fight the war without worrying about their loved ones. But, balanced against those feelings, yet to come into outright conflict with them, were calls for the election of certain officers and for political matters to be discussed by the army. The *nature* of the war became the question, with soldiers concerned that the generals would use a defensive war to try to resurrect the Tsar's regime.

It is not surprising that soldiers and workers in Russia held contradictory ideas. Their revolution as yet still hadn't overcome the contradictions of capitalism, and ideas are rooted in reality. The vast majority were not initially anti-war. The idea of fighting a war for democracy and liberty fitted well with the sentiments behind overthrowing the Tsar. But the act of ridding Russia of its monarchy gave people a sense of how society can be changed, and when the Provisional government refused to stop the war that was creating hardship it failed to stop the momentum for revolutionary change.

Mutiny

The duration and horror of the war, the ineptitude of the generals, the plummeting living standards, all fed into a crisis of nationalism. But it was the example of the Russian Revolution that opened up new possibilities for change. The revolutionary transformation of society now became a viable option in workers' and soldiers' minds.

The February Revolution transformed the resistance to the war. It became less piecemeal and more widespread and unified. The notion that the workers, peasants and soldiers of Russia had wrought such momentous change against their rulers, and therefore had potentially endangered their war effort, had an enormous impact. The strike figures in Britain, France and Italy jumped significantly in 1917. The first major illustration of the impact of revolution on soldiers followed the overthrow of the Tsar in February 1917. Mutinies escalated as war weariness increased. And it was the French army that provided the 'greatest of all crises that Europe saw in the war before the October Revolution'.[77]

Unsurprisingly, given the level of slaughter at Verdun, the area between Paris and Verdun was the most affected by mutiny. In the two weeks immediately preceding the mutiny, more than 250,000 French soldiers had died to gain 500 yards of ground in the Chemin de Dames. In April 1917 entire units refused to go back up the line, protesting against bad conditions and against the offensive. The mutinies mushroomed. Between April and September, an estimated 500,000 soldiers were affected, 68 divisions—over half the divisions in the French army—in 151 recorded incidents.[78] Desertions from the front went up from an average of 1,437 to 2,625 in 1917 and from the rear they increased from an average of 15,745 to 27,579.[79]

Many wanted to march on Paris, chanted 'Down with the war' and sang the Internationale. In some units, the idea of creating soviets was discussed. In May, mutineers from the 36th and 129th regiments met and composed a resolution: 'We want peace...we've had enough of the war and we want the deputies to know it... When we go into the trenches, we will plant a white flag on the parapet. The Germans will do the same, and we will not fight until the peace is signed'.[80] Mutinous soldiers made connections with civilian workers: 'I am ready to go into the trenches, but we are doing like the clothing workers. We are going out on strike,' wrote one soldier.[81] In June, two Russian brigades were moved to a camp at La Courtine, 200 miles south of Paris. They quickly established a soviet, involving French soldiers,

> by the end of July the 10,000 men at La Courtine were heading for open revolt... 'Down with the war!' said a notice over the door of the delegates' hut. Passing round the units was a proclamation from Russia, 'Declaration of the Soldiers' Rights', which advocated extreme liberty of speech and revolution.[82]

The same month, the Commission d'Armée met in Paris, to be told by Deputy Abel Ferry that 'demoralisation is gripping the French army. It is with a heavy heart that I have to tell you that a regiment has revolted...that in several others military policemen have been attacked and hanged, and in the leave-trains soldiers are openly singing the Internationale!'[83]

After the revolts were put down, military tribunals found 3,427 soldiers guilty of mutiny—554 were sentenced to death, and 49 actually shot. For such an immense movement, the punishment was limited. The mutinies terrified the French generals and the ruling class. The French general Nivelle (widely held responsible for the bloodbath at Chemin de Dames) was replaced by Pétain as a sop to the soldiers. The overthrow of the regime in Russia was no doubt uppermost in the minds of the French establishment. The argument that, as a victor in the war, France experienced little of the revolutionary feeling seen in Russia discounts the potential revealed in these revolts. One writer, not especially sympathetic to mutiny or revolution, argues that 'France had narrowly avoided a revolution'.[84] 'The summer of 1917 severely shook the confidence of ruling classes, with mutinies and strikes reviving and the Russian Revolution taking effect'.[85] In February 1917 in France Nivelle had complained of 'the Army's being infested with pamphlets, it is a veritable epidemic'.[86] The generals blamed the mutinies of April not on the disastrous Chemin de Dames campaign but on agents provocateurs and socialists.

Mutinies were not confined to the French army, however. In September 1917 there were five days of disorder among British troops at Etaples base camp. Etaples was notorious for its brutal regime and bullying officers. An article in the *Workers Dreadnought* of 30 September carried a report from a participant in the mutiny: 'About four weeks ago about 10,000 men had a big racket at Etaples and cleared the place from one end to the other, and when the General asked what was wrong, they said they wanted the war stopped'.[87]

In 1917 there were 48,282 mutineers in the Italian army, and 56,268 deserters. The numbers kept rising; between May and October there were 24,000 new mutineers or deserters.[88] Mutinies were met with increasing repression—359 soldiers were executed in 1917, compared to 66 in 1915. 'In September 1917 there was no counting the number of times soldiers refused to march'.[89]

In October 1917 the Italian army were humiliated at Caporetto: although the Central Powers did not significantly outnumber the Italian troops, it turned into a rout. The Central Powers took 293,000 prisoners and occupied the area around Venice losing no more than a handful of men. But Caporetto was not simply a military disaster. There was an element of anti-war consciousness involved: 200,000 men surrendered, refusing to fight. Captain Rommel, leading the central forces, wrote of the Italian soldiers' response to his invitation to surrender:

> *Suddenly the mass began to move and, in the ensuing panic, swept its resisting officers along downhill. Most of the soldiers threw their weapons away and hundreds hurried to me… An Italian officer who hesitated to surrender was shot down by his own troops. For the Italians on Mrzli peak the*

war was over. They shouted with joy.[90]

In Germany the collapse of Tsarism removed the right wing Social Democrats' 'excuse' that the war was directed against Russian tyranny. It became increasingly obvious to the German people that the aims of industrialists were expansionist: they wanted to push into Belgium and France and exercise 'hegemony' over Eastern and Central Europe.[91] In April 1917 a strike of 200,000 metal workers was led by militants opposed to the war: 'Spontaneous unrest over food shortages was beginning to merge with political opposition to the war'.[92] Between June 1917 and January 1918 there was a series of mutinies at Kiel among the fleet

Revolutionary forces unleashed

After the February Revolution in Russia, the Provisional government that had replaced the Tsar continued to prosecute the war 'more efficiently', while telling the workers and peasants that significant change could not come until the war was over, therefore stoking the anti-war feeling of the masses. The government wanted a war that would divide and exhaust the revolution. But those fighting the war had had enough. War weariness was endemic. Soldiers revolted; deserting, lynching officers they didn't like. Discipline slipped away. After February, the Petrograd Soviet issued Order No 1, which effectively created dual power within the armed services: committees of elected soldiers were set up and the orders of the government were to be obeyed only if they did not conflict with those of the Soviet. All hierarchical titles were scrapped. Soldiers and officers were to share the same rights once they returned to civilian life.

Despite several attempts by Kerensky's government to modify this, the reality of dual power simply fed the crisis in the armed forces. The disintegration of the Russian army accelerated. 'By October 1917 some 2 million solders had deserted—mostly between February and October'.[93] Kerensky bowed to the generals' demand to restore the death penalty for desertion at the front, although, as one remarked: 'Is it really possible to execute entire divisions?' Soldiers were, due to their hatred of the war, moving towards the Bolsheviks' position on the war. The figures regarding the influence of the Bolsheviks in the armed forces speak volumes about the ideological shifts taking place in the army:

The total number of Bolsheviks in the army at the time of the February Revolution was a couple of thousand. By the time of the April Conference it had risen to 6,000, and on 16 June it was 26,000. After that soldiers in practically all corps, divisions, batteries and other units began to join the party.

*On 5 October, on the north western front alone, there were 48,994 party
members and 7,452 candidates. On 15 October, on the northern front there
were 13,000 party members.*[94]

Bolshevik influence spread beyond the army: the peasants were drawn
into the revolution, the nationalities' movement was growing and the
Provisional government was increasingly paralysed by events. The
Bolsheviks gained the majority in the Petrograd Soviet and, on 25
October, the Bolsheviks led an insurrection to seize power. Immediately
after the October insurrection, the Bolsheviks published the secret treaties
that had provoked the war and renounced the imperial possessions of
Russia. They proposed peace to all nations involved in the war, peace not
as a way of doing a deal with the capitalist nations, but as a weapon. 'If
the unlikely happens,' Lenin argued, 'then none of the states will accept
an armistice, and we shall be able to call this war just, and defensive.
Russia will become the ally of the world's proletariat, of all the oppressed
of the globe'.[95]

To this end, the party began to organise among German soldiers at the
Eastern Front, publishing a newspaper to circulate among the troops,
calling on them to make the German revolution and end the war on both
fronts. The Allies, rather than accept peace, threw themselves into aiding
the enemies of the revolution. Counter-revolutionary Russian generals
were backed by Britain and Romania. The Allied war council agreed in
June 1918 that each country was to send 4,000-5,000 troops to 'support
the Whites'.[96] The Central Powers supported anti-Bolshevik movements
in Georgia, the Ukraine and Finland.

The Bolshevik Revolution united the ruling classes who, until then,
had been at each other's throats. The possibility of the spread of revolution was an immediate threat to their entire system, and a greater danger
than the predatory ambitions of rival states. A German newspaper
described it this way: 'The struggle against Bolshevism must force the
three Allied powers and their enemies together. A strong Germany will
resist Bolshevism, whereas, if she succumbed to it, the worst kind of revolution would annihilate Europe'.[97] Churchill agreed: 'We might have to
build up the German army, as it was important to get Germany on her
legs again for fear of the spread of Bolshevism'.[98] The French leader
Clemenceau said, 'This new and monstrous form of imperialism will
threaten Europe all the more…as it comes precisely at the end of the war,
which will inevitably provoke, in all countries, a serious economic and
social crisis… The Allies must therefore cause the soviets to collapse'.[99]
The war was now as much a crusade against the Russian Revolution as it
was an expansionist conflict.

Yet it was not straightforward to get Allied troops to fight in Russia.
There was widespread disaffection with the slowness of demobilisation

after the Armistice was signed on 11 November 1918. Soldiers who had fought in France and expected to return home to a heroes' welcome found themselves being sent to fight a former ally with precious little explanation. It was not a popular or successful operation; even the *Daily Express* printed an editorial declaring that 'the frozen plains of Eastern Europe are not worth the bones of a single British grenadier'.[100]

Allied soldiers landed at Murmansk in Northern Russia in February 1918, and more followed in April and May. The intention was to provide support and training for the White armies fighting the Bolsheviks. The occupying forces went so far as to set up an anti-Soviet government at Archangel. But British soldiers didn't need a lot of convincing that fighting the Bolsheviks was not the reason they had signed up. Bolshevik leaflets that argued the Allied invasion meant that British soldiers were fighting against the revolution and therefore against the work of their own working class touched a chord. The socialist paper *The Call*, which was circulated behind British and US lines, made it clear that the Bolsheviks had proposed peace.

During 1918 and 1919 there were mutinies of British soldiers at Archangel, Kem, Kandalaksha, Murmansk, Onega and Seletskoi near the front line. In February 1919 a private stationed at Seletskoi reported in a letter, 'All have gone on strike—held meetings last night and passed resolutions that they must be withdrawn from Russia immediately'.[101] The White generals were enlisted to support the British officers in keeping control of the troops. One of them, V V Maruchevsky, described the situation afterwards: '[the Yorkshires] organised a mutiny, and it seems, this developed into a strong wish to stop fighting. The English have concealed all this very thoroughly, but I came to know of this episode through a despatch from Colonel Micheva, who, at the request of the local British command, positioned machine guns on the road in case of open riot by the British'.[102]

In March 1919 Lieutenant-Colonel Radcliffe, Assistant Director of Military Operations, reported to the Deputy Chief of the Imperial General Staff concerning the 'unreliable state of the troops [in Archangel and Murmansk].' They were 'tired, dispirited, homesick and inclined to be mutinous', as well as being receptive to 'very active and insidious Bolshevik propaganda'.[103] There were two mutinies in six weeks in November and December 1918 at Archangel among those Russian soldiers supposed to form the North Russian [White] National Army. Between April and June 1919 there were a number of mutinies among the North Russian Rifles.

At Onega on 20 July, in an extraordinary example of how tenuous was the loyalty the White generals could command, men from the 5th North Russian Rifles and the Archangel regiment murdered their officers. About

100 declined to join the Red Army, some deserted, but the bulk—over 600 men—stayed and fought alongside the Red Army in a nine hour battle against Allied-supported White forces. Even more demoralising for the Whites and the Allies, there was a mutiny among the over 4,000 men who made up the elite Slavo-British Legion. The unit had been seen as the most trustworthy, containing those soldiers most loyal to the counter-revolution. As Lawrence James writes, 'The British could create and train crack units like the Slavo-British Legion, but its officers could not give the men who served in them a cause to fight for'.[104] The Bolsheviks could, and many of the 4,000 joined the Red forces.

The July mutinies were the final nail in the coffin of British participation in the Allied invasion of North Russia. Churchill, secretary for war, was dismayed by the events and, by October, the 18,000 British troops were evacuated. As early as January, Churchill had written to Lloyd George pushing to continue the intervention, yet saying, 'unfortunately we have not the power—our orders would not be obeyed, I regret to say'.[105] Lenin wrote in January, 'Attempts to conquer Russia, which require a long term occupation army of a million men, are the most certain road to the most rapid extension of proletarian revolution to the Entente countries'.[106] This was a point not lost on the Entente ruling classes.

The Bolsheviks' intervention at the Brest-Litovsk peace negotiations with the Germans in December 1917 had a real impact on the struggle. Though the 'German military establishment saw the Russian offer of peace as a chance to expand the German empire still further... The Russian negotiators were appealing as much to the German workers as the high Command.' Trotsky and Karl Radek, a revolutionary who had been active in Germany before the war, arrived at Brest-Litovsk and 'Radek, before the eyes of the diplomats and officials assembled on the platform to greet them, began to distribute pamphlets among the German soldiers'.[107] In January 1918 strikes shook Austria-Hungary. In Vienna workers' councils were established. In Germany, at the Spartakists' call, 400,000 struck in Berlin on 28 January. The movement was smashed, with many sent to t..e front, but the strikes, like the Kiel protests, were a beginning.

In the summer of 1918 the German army launched a massive attack on the Western Front. With the withdrawal of Russia, there was no need to defend the Eastern Front, so they could concentrate all their resources in France. Against the odds, the Allies began to roll the Germans back at the Marne, and—completely unexpectedly—the Central Powers looked to be heading to defeat. Military disaster coincided with a food crisis at home. While the poor starved, the rich were provided for via the black market, further stoking class tensions.

On 8 August at Amiens, thousands of Germans surrendered almost without a fight—and Ludendorff, who headed the military regime, resigned. In quick succession, the centre collapsed. The Austrians caved in on 26 September: the army in pieces, the king abdicated. Bulgaria surrendered on 18 September. The Habsburg empire was disintegrating. The Czech Republic was proclaimed on 29 October, Hungary declared independence and Yugoslavia was formed. On 30 October armed workers and soldiers seized government buildings in Budapest, declaring Hungary's withdrawal from the war.

Returning soldiers were 'highly organised, disciplined...ready to fight.' They were also armed. One study in Germany 'noted with alarm that 1,895,052 rifles, 8,452 machine guns and 4,000 trench mortars had been "lost" by the army on retreat'.[108]

On 3 November revolution broke out in Vienna, and the German Revolution began with a mutiny at Kiel—the sailors refused to fight an obviously suicidal battle 'for honour's sake'. The sailors involved were arrested, provoking a demonstration by thousands more sailors through the town. In a matter of days, revolution swept Germany. Workers' councils sprang up all over the country. On 9 November Prince Max resigned and handed power to the right wing social democrat Ebert. Together the SPD member and the monarchist announced the abdication of the Kaiser, who fled to Holland. Soldiers could not be relied on to put down the revolution. 'The Kaiser Alexander regiment has gone over to the revolution; the soldiers had rushed out of the barracks gates and fraternised with the shouting crowd outside; men shook their hands with emotion and girls stuck flowers in their uniforms and embraced them...officers are being stripped of their cockades and gold lace'.[109] The German empire was in tatters. The war was over.

It was not simply weariness or anger at the slaughter that had revolutionised so many soldiers. In addition to the experience shared in the trenches, ordinary soldiers shared a common disillusionment with the civilian life they returned to 'often shattered under the impact of demobilisation, unemployment, poverty and the sheer strangeness of what was once familiar'.[110]

War changes people, but so does revolution. An interesting feature of the German Revolution was the impact that it had on the psychology of individuals. Many men had returned from the war suffering a variety of war neuroses: anxiety, 'shell shock', mental disturbances. Kurt Singer, a director of the neuropsychiatric ward of a Berlin hospital, witnessed a mass recovery in November. 'With the beginning of the revolution, 20 patients abandoned the ward without leave, six asked for immediate release and the remaining ten stayed, Singer suspected, only because they were waiting for warmer weather'.[111] Singer described the shift in consciousness from war weariness and despair to revolutionary fervour and hope:

The revolution itself terminated the need for the neurotic complex as a protest of the inferior, the suppressed, the subordinated, precisely for that class of men who made up the main contingent of neurotics—the uniformed working proletariat. These compensations for the feelings of inferiority...were, suddenly, no longer necessary once the existing power relations were so radically transformed.[112]

Even in countries where revolution did not break through, there were huge struggles. France, Italy and Czechoslovakia saw the growth of mass Communist parties as the Russian Revolution inspired workers around the world. Britain and Italy were in a pre-revolutionary situation.

For the last year of the war, Italian industrialisation took off on a massive scale. The working class grew enormously. Trade unions grew to 3 million members. The end of the war brought no increased territory for Italy. The bitterness felt in the aftermath of war coupled with the explosion of working class growth polarised politics in Italy. The fascists under Mussolini emerged on the one hand, but on the other workers' revolutionary militancy exploded in the two red years, the *biennio rosso*. In 1919 and 1920 huge strikes built into factory occupations. 'In Turin the factory occupations took on elements of "dual power", as working class power organised through factory councils opposed that of the official government. Armed workers defended the factories and the elected factory councils took on the nature of soviets in the city'.[113] Agricultural workers also struck for land reform and organised themselves into red leagues. To prevent the very real danger of revolution sweeping away their privileges and profits, the industrialists and landowners looked to the armed fascists—the army could not be relied on. The factory occupations ended in late September 1920. As soon as it was clear that the struggle was ebbing, the Blackshirts 'conducted a systematic campaign of terror against the socialists and their local institutions'.[114]

In Britain there were serious strikes and mutinies of soldiers angry at the slow speed of demobilisation after the Armistice. As already described, there was resistance to fighting in Russia. Soldiers wanted to get back to their lives and the promised 'homes fit for heroes'. One soldier, Sergeant Buckeridge, wrote in November 1918: 'It seemed as though the whole army had become imbued with a spirit of revolt against the system which had held the individual so firmly for so long'.[115]

In January 1919, 10,000 soldiers demonstrated at Folkestone against being sent back to France. They set up a soldiers' union and refused to sail. At Dover, 2,000 soldiers struck. Protests spread across Britain during January. Some 20,000 British soldiers mutinied at Calais— electing strike committees and a soldiers' council. Churchill wrote that 'under the present pressure the army is liquefying fast'.[116] He cabled Lloyd George, the prime minister, that, if demobilisation were not speeded up, there would be nothing left of the army but a 'demoralised and angry mob'.[117] Haig complained that if things went on in the same vein he would have no army left in France by February.

The ruling class were faced with a double problem: not only could they not get soldiers to fight, neither could they confidently use troops against strikers. And they needed to. Britain came close to revolution between January and March 1919. The experience of revolution in Russia and central Europe fed into disillusionment with life after the war when the privations of wartime continued: 'shortages of food, housing...now aggravated by rapid price rises, unemployment, snail's pace demobilisation of men from the forces and, to add insult to injury, the conspicuous luxury enjoyed by the war profiteers'.[118] Demanding a 40 hour week, 100,000 workers struck in Glasgow. Miners struck, rail workers struck, sailors mutinied and even the police went on strike. The British ruling class were on the defensive—Bonar Law told Lloyd George that even 'The King is in a funk about the labour situation and is talking about the...danger of revolution'.[119]

In the absence of a party like the Bolsheviks the struggles were contained, but it was yet another symbol of the fire the Russian Revolution had lit all over Europe. Victor Serge described yet more convulsions,

> Riots in Paris, riots in Lyon, revolution in Belgium, revolution in Constantinople, victory of the soviets in Bulgaria, rioting in Copenhagen. In fact the whole of Europe is in movement, clandestine or open soviets are appearing everywhere, even in the Allied armies; everything is possible, everything.[120]

Lenin declared that the 'world revolution is beginning', and was echoed by Lloyd George, who said 'the whole of Europe is filled with the spirit of revolution.'

Revolutionary defeatism

In 1914 such dramatic events seemed a lifetime away. For revolutionary internationalists the outbreak of war brought a double blow. The despair at millions of workers marching off to be slaughtered and the seeming vice-like hold of nationalism was matched by horror at the betrayal of the forces of international socialism. The French writer Romain Rolland spoke for all those who had placed their faith in the International by describing its collapse as 'the greatest catastrophe in history...the ruin of our most sacred hopes for human fraternity'.[121]

The left began to re-emerge despite the havoc wreaked on socialist organisations by mobilisation and the intense pressure from national ruling classes for socialists to support the war. As protest grew, socialists in Serbia, Greece, Bulgaria, Switzerland, Spain and Germany began to raise their voices against the barbarity. Yet their numbers and influence was small. The Bolshevik party was one of a tiny number of organisations that managed a consistent record of resistance to the war. As early as July 1914, Lenin had drafted an article called 'War and Revolution', in which he argued the 'best war against war is revolution'.[122] He moved to Switzerland in September and presented his 'Theses on the War' to the handful of fellow Bolsheviks. Lenin's key points were that the war was an imperialist conflict; that the betrayal of the main socialist parties signalled the 'ideological collapse of the International'; that the key task for the Bolsheviks was to continue the struggle against Tsarism whether in wartime or not; and that therefore socialists should break from the defunct Second International and agitate among their respective working classes to end the war through revolution. This would entail rejecting the *Burgfrieden*, encouraging soldiers' fraternisation and protests, and urging workers to fight their own governments whatever the military consequences. Lenin's position meant taking an unpopular stand against the war with initially little likelihood of winning much support. Nonetheless, Lenin was clear that a principled position was crucial if revolutionaries were to resist the opportunism of the Second International and be able to lead revolutionary struggles that would, almost surely, emerge from the war. It was a long term perspective, summarised thus: 'In all advanced countries the war has placed on the order of the day the slogan of socialist revolution…the conversion of the present imperialist war into a civil war is the only correct proletarian slogan.'

For Lenin, breaking the ideological hold the ruling class maintained meant breaking the idea of national defence and adopting an internationalist working class perspective:

> *Present day socialism will remain true to itself only if it joins neither one nor the other imperialist bourgeoisie, only if it says that the two sides are 'both worse', and if it wishes the defeat of the imperialist bourgeoisie in every country. Any other decision will, in reality, be national-liberal and have nothing in common with genuine internationalism.*
>
> *A revolutionary class cannot but wish for the defeat of its government in a reactionary war, and cannot fail to see that the latter's military reverses must facilitate its overthrow…the socialists of **all** the belligerent countries should express their wish that all their 'own' governments should be defeated.*[123]

Lenin's 'Theses on the War' provide a clarity unmatched by any other contribution to anti-war writing but it contained arguments that were deeply controversial within the internationalist left. In Russia, many Bolsheviks rejected Lenin's argument that 'from the point of view of the labouring class and the toiling masses of all the Russian people, the lesser evil would be a defeat for the Tsarist monarchy'.[124] But in the context it sliced through the abstractions and vagaries of many other socialists who were desperate not to alienate the masses. Against an insurrectionary solution to war, other socialist parties posed slogans which failed to address the class contradictions at the heart of the war; the Menshevik Martov called for 'peace', while the Socialist Revolutionary Victor Chernov adopted the deeply ambiguous slogan 'neither victory nor defeat'. Let everything return to the pre-war status quo— despite the fact that the pre-war crisis led to the holocaust in the first place! Lenin was uncompromising. 'The slogan of peace is in my mind incorrect, our slogan must be civil war,' he wrote:

> All arguments to the effect that this slogan is unworkable, etc, etc, are pure sophism. We cannot 'make' it, but we propagate for it and work in this direction. In every country one must struggle first of all against **one's own** proper chauvinism, awaken hatred for **one's own** regime, call (repeatedly, persistently, ever again, tirelessly) for solidarity among the workers of the warring nations. No one is proposing to **guarantee** when and to what degree this work will prove practicable or justified: **This is not what is at issue**. At issue is the **line** of work. **Only** such work is socialist and not chauvinist. And it **alone** will bear socialist fruit, revolutionary fruit.[125]

As the left began to raise its head, it was clear that the opposition movement must move beyond small factions and fight for its position within the mass working class parties, especially the SPD. In December, Karl Liebnecht voted against war credits, and by extension, against the false unity in the SPD. His actions made him the bitter enemy of the right wing social democrats but, according to a begrudging Kautsky, also made him 'the most popular man in the trenches'.[126] Increasingly, popular disaffection with the war grew and the Bolsheviks led the international revolutionary opposition to it.

Lenin was key to forcing this momentum forward. He linked his analysis of the war and the response revolutionaries should take to it with the argument that the war should be the midwife of a new International, cleansed of opportunism. As he wrote to the Bolshevik Shliapnikov, 'Our task is now an absolute and open struggle with international opportunism… This is an international task. It rests upon us, for there is no one else. We cannot put it aside'.[127]

In September 1915, 38 internationalist delegates from 11 different countries and with different positions regarding the war met at Zimmerwald in Switzerland. The conference was called by moderate socialists to restore the idea that the International was a force for peace. Lenin and Radek uncompromisingly advocated a break with the leadership of the Second International. They argued that any continued connection to the Second International leaders like Ebert, Scheidemann and Guesde could only disorient and disarm the workers.

The majority of delegates were reluctant to make such a stand. Neither would they support Lenin's theory of the necessity of turning the imperialist war into a civil war between classes by encouraging strikes and revolts within each country against their respective ruling classes. The manifesto that came out of the first Zimmerwald conference merely stated that the war was an imperialist one, fought for profit and greed, that the declarations of the capitalist class that the war was being fought for democracy and the liberty of oppressed nations was a lie, and that instead 'new chains, new burdens are being brought into existence, and the workers of all countries, of the victorious as well as the of the vanquished, will have to bear them.' It criticised the role of the socialist parties' leaders who 'have invited the workers to suspend the working class struggle, the only possible and effective means of working class emancipation'. However, there was no mention of directing that struggle concretely against the warmongers. Instead, the task was 'to take up this fight for peace—for a peace without annexations or war indemnities'.[128]

These formulations were abstract—and by accepting the idea of peace without annexations the manifesto's signatories accepted that capitalist institutions could bring a just peace. The Bolsheviks signed the Zimmerwald declaration, because Lenin saw it as 'a step towards an ideological and practical break with opportunism and social-chauvinism',[129] despite arguing bitterly with its conclusions.

Lenin could now look to groups in Germany, France, Britain, the Netherlands, Sweden, Bulgaria and Italy who agreed on the need to break from the Second International. Lenin concluded that 'to rally together these Marxist elements, no matter how small they might be at first…here is the task at hand'.[130] Trotsky later described Lenin's intervention as 'laying the cornerstone of the revolutionary International'.[131] Zimmerwald did indeed have a resonance among socialists in warring countries. It sent up a flare that illuminated a way out of political isolation for those who opposed the war in every belligerent nation.

The second Zimmerwald conference took place against the background of the continuing mayhem at Verdun and increasing economic strain on the belligerent nations. Held at Kienthal in Switzerland in April 1916, seven nations were represented by 43 delegates. Many more had been refused visas to travel to the conference. Again the Zimmerwald left put forward the necessity of breaking with the opportunists of the Second International and advocated the slogan of revolutionary defeatism against the utopian search for a democratic peace under capitalism. 'The mirage of a "democratic" peace' would 'represent nothing more than an agreement between imperialist bandits...and increase the menace of new wars...to summon the proletariat to struggle and organise it for a resolute attack upon capitalism—this is the only peace programme of social democracy'.[132]

Kienthal was another step on the road to pulling sections of the left towards Lenin's position and in the months between the conference and the outbreak of the February Revolution in Russia the Zimmerwald left gained ground. There were huge May Day demonstrations in 1916. In Berlin 10,000 gathered to protest at the war and Liebnecht was arrested. As the third year of the war wore on, a rising tide of unrest across Europe confirmed for Lenin that there were increasingly 'two Internationals' competing for the hearts and minds of workers. Either the Zimmerwald movement would split from the Second International or it would be left behind.

In Germany, the SPD was in decline. Its membership fell by 63 percent between August 1914 and 1916; the left were exerting more pressure on the right wing of the party and its national conference in 1916 was rocked by dissent over its position on the war. The great schism was only months away—the Independent Social Democrats (USPD), a left and centre grouping which included the Spartakus League, split from the party in January 1917. The SPD monolith was cracking down the middle. In France, despite considerable abuse, three deputies voted against war credits in June. In Italy, Austria and in Sweden debates over the direction of the main socialist parties reflected the changing political climate. The common picture was of defencist majorities clinging precariously to control of the party machines, but everywhere centrist and revolutionary oppositions gained ground. 'In every significant national movement a left radical faction aligned with Lenin's position had come into being... The Zimmerwald left tendency was well on the way to becoming a movement...due to the process of division set into motion by the policy of 4 August'.[133]

In the months before February 1917, Lenin continued to develop his theory of revolutionary defeatism. As the political situation developed, it was clear that revolutionary defeatism was the cornerstone for forging a real revolutionary activity. A thousand threads ran from it; arguments on the national question, on the nature of the war, social democracy and the possibility of revolutionary change. In his debates with the Swiss moderates in the Zimmerwald movement Lenin made the nature of revolutionary change yet more concrete. While the moderates would not rule out support for militarism if Switzerland were to enter the war, justifying their stand by dismissing the possibility of revolution, Lenin was arguing against pacifism, stressing the necessity for force in ending the violence of capitalism. Throughout, Lenin's aim was to forge a revolutionary current distinguished by political clarity and strength of purpose.

The antagonism between the moderates and the left within Zimmerwald was rendering it hopelessly divided. Lenin wrote to Inessa Armand that, 'There it is, my fate. One fighting campaign after another...against political stupidity, opportunism, philistinism, etc.' So weary with the bickering and rivalry was he that at times he seemed despairing at the size of the task. Famously, at a conference of Swiss socialist youth in January 1917, he remarked, 'We elders, perhaps, may not live to see the decisive battles...of the approaching proletarian revolution'.[134] He was wrong. The February Revolution erupted and decisively altered the course of history. R Craig Nation, a historian of the Zimmerwald movement, describes how, 'In the pale light of the northern winter the masses, so often invoked as an abstraction by the Marxist left, stepped forward as a living, revolutionary force. The army mutinied, the people armed, the Tsar deposed, the proletariat in the vanguard—it was a vindication of the line that Lenin defended almost alone during the first days of the war'.[135]

Revolutionary defeatism was more relevant than ever after February. When Lenin returned to Russia, he saw clearly that the revolution was partial and needed to go beyond the limits of parliamentary democracy if it was to end the war and bring real liberation. Breaking the ideas of revolutionary defencism—the idea that the revolution changed the nature of the war, and that defence of Russia was a defence of the aims of the revolution—was a central task for revolutionary socialists if the revolution was to progress to an overthrow of capitalism itself. The role of the Bolsheviks in explaining the true nature of the war was key to this process:

> The bourgeoisie deceives the people by working on their noble pride in the revolution and by pretending that the **social and political** character of the war, as far as Russia was concerned, underwent a change because of this stage of the revolution... What is required of us is the **ability** to explain to the masses that the social and political character of the war is determined not by the 'good will' of individuals or groups, or even of nations, but by the position of the **class** which conducts the war, by the class **policy** of which the war is a continuation, by the ties of **capital**, which is the dominant economic force in modern society, by the **imperialist character** of international capital...and so on.[136]

Actually stopping the war would require a further transformation of society, partially made possible by the shifts in consciousness on the part of the workers and soldiers. The establishment of soviets, which concretely bridged the gap between politics and economics, meant the mechanism existed for workers to begin ruling themselves. Lenin argued: 'The Russian Revolution of February-March 1917 was the beginning of the transformation of the imperialist war into a civil war. This revolution took the *first* step towards ending the war; but it requires a *second* step, namely, the transfer of state power to the proletariat, to make the end of the war a *certainty*'.[137]

The success of the October Revolution unequivocally demonstrated that the Bolsheviks, trained through nearly four years of war to wage arguments against the war and for revolution in sometimes very hostile circumstances, were the only force organised, disciplined and politically clear enough to have won respect and influence in the working class and so lead it to victory. The theory of revolutionary defeatism, fought for and won within the party and the class was a crucial weapon in the party's political arsenal.[138]

Conclusion

Rather than remember the First World War as our rulers do—with pious hypocrisy and poppies every November—socialists can look back, learn and be inspired. The period from 1914 to 1919 was a tremendous turning point in human history. The barbarity of capitalism was unleashed in a way previously undreamt of; millions of lives were lost, millions more wrecked forever. The First World War was the terrible infant of capitalism. The nature of imperialism and of war was revealed in all its naked horror. But those few years also brought the clearest example to date of the alternative to such bloodshed. The Russian Revolution raised a beacon that millions looked to around the world. It sparked revolution in Germany, in Austria, in Hungary, and ignited powerful clashes with the state in Italy and Britain. It was a testing time for revolutionary socialists in all those countries—the point at which the old socialist parties proved themselves to be counter-revolutionary and true internationalists had to fight for ideological clarity under the most difficult circumstances. In forging that clarity, Lenin and his supporters were fighting for a vision of the future that went beyond socialism in one country. As Nation argues:

> That vision, still inchoate prior to 1914, had grown in the course of the war into an integrated theory, embodied by the Zimmerwald left and its challenge to the Second International. On the eve of the February Revolution the challenge was fully matured. Though the explosion in Russia gave Lenin's cause a huge push forward, the elements that would combine to create an autonomous communist left between 1917 and 1921 were already in place prior to the Tsar's abdication. International communism did not spring from the 'accident' of revolution, nor was it ever a simple extension of the Bolsheviks' fight to seize and maintain state power. Its roots lay in the left opposition's reaction to the socialist collapse of 1914 and the international movement of protest against the world war that followed.[139]

The youth and inexperience of many of the new Communist parties was a key factor in the ability of capitalism to douse of the flames of revolution. Revolutionary organisations rooted in the working classes of Britain and Italy, and especially in Germany, could have been decisive. Yet, despite this lack and the impact on the world working class of the failure of that revolutionary wave, the First World War years remain a crucial time in which attitudes to nationalism, to imperialism, to reformism, and to revolution were hammered out in the heat of class battle. They were years in which significant numbers of workers moved from patriotism to revolution and began the process of taking control of society and their own lives.

Notes

1   J Winter and B Blaggett, *1914-18* (BBC Books, 1996), p10.
2   E J Hobsbawm, *The Age of Extremes* (London, 1994), p31.
3   M Ferro, *The Great War 1914-1918* (London, 1973), p130.
4   Ibid, p227.
5   M Gilbert, *First World War* (London, 1995), p541.
6   E J Hobsbawm, op cit, p26.
7   Ibid, p25.
8   J Winter and B Blaggett, op cit, p69.
9   Ibid, p157.
10 E J Hobsbawm, op cit, p26.
11 M Gilbert, op cit, p299.
12 General Sir Alfred Knox, quoted in J Rees, 'In Defence of October', *International Socialism* 52, p11.
13 E J Hobsbawm, *The Age of Extremes*, op cit, p51.
14 J Winter and B Blaggett, op cit, p362.
15 Ibid, p31.
16 E J Hobsbawm, *The Age of Empire* (London, 1987), p317.
17 See Lenin's description of this process, quoted in T Cliff, *Lenin*, vol 2 (London, 1985), p3.
18 C Harman, *The Lost Revolution* (London, 1997), p21.
19 J Ellis, *The Social History of the Machine Gun* (Pimlico, 1993), p113.
20 E J Hobsbawm, *The Age of Extremes*, op cit, p45.
21 C Harman, 'The Return of the National Question', *International Socialism* 56, p15.
22 E J Hobsbawm, *The Age of Empire*, op cit, p323.
23 Ibid, p321.
24 B Pearce and M Woodhouse, *A History of Communism in Britain* (London, 1995), p117.
25 E J Leed, *No Man's Land: Combat and Identity in World War One* (Cambridge, 1979), p40.
26 Cited in E J Hobsbawm, *The Age of Extremes*, op cit, p325, and in M Ferro, op cit, p8.
27 E J Hobsbawm, *The Age of Empire*, op cit, p326.
28 T Cliff, op cit, p26.
29 E J Hobsbawm, *The Age of Empire*, op cit, p325.
30 E J Leed, op cit, p40.

31   E J Leed, op cit, p66.
32   L Trotsky, *My Life* (Penguin, 1975), p240.
33   Quoted in E J Leed, op cit, p40.
34   J Winter and B Blaggett, op cit, p248.
35   A Rothstein, *The Soldiers' Strikes 1919* (London, 1980), p10.
36   E J Leed, op cit, p1.
37   Ibid, p76.
38   Ibid, p84.
39   Ibid.
40   Ibid, p86.
41   Ibid, p88.
42   Ibid, p89.
43   Ibid.
44   J Winter and B Blaggett, op cit, p97.
45   E J Leed, op cit, p89.
46   T Ashworth, *Trench Warfare 1914-1918, the Live and Let Live System* (Macmillan, 1980), p13.
47   M Ferro, op cit, p178.
48   Quoted in T Cliff, op cit, p30.
49   Ibid.
50   M Ferro, op cit, p173.
51   C Harman, *The Lost Revolution*, op cit, p28.
52   D Gluckstein, *The Western Soviets* (London, 1985), p70.
53   M Ferro, op cit, p201.
54   Ibid, p200.
55   Ibid, p170.
56   E J Leed, op cit, p95.
57   L Trotsky, op cit, p241.
58   E J Hobsbawm, *Nations and Nationalism* (Cambridge, 1990), p127.
59   Ibid, p124.
60   Ibid, p130.
61   M Ferro, op cit, p213.
62   E J Hobsbawm, *Nations and Nationalism*, op cit, p130.
63   E J Leed, op cit, p198.
64   S F Kissin, *War and the Marxists* (London, 1988), p158.
65   Ibid, p170.
66   C Schorske, *German Social Democracy 1905-1917* (Cambridge, Massachusetts, 1983), p289.
67   Ibid, p290.
68   Quoted in R C Nation, *War on War* (Duke University Press, 1989), p24.
69   S F Kissin, op cit, p162.
70   M Ferro, op cit, p160.
71   Ibid, p158.
72   Quoted in B Pearce and M Woodhouse, op cit, p117.
73   Quoted in R C Nation, op cit, p25.
74   N Stone, *The Eastern Front 1914-17* (Purnell Book Club, 1975), p285.
75   M Ferro, op cit, p178.
76   Ibid, p187.
77   M Ferro, op cit, p181.
78   T Ashworth, op cit, p224.
79   J Williams, *Mutiny 1917* (Heinemann, 1962), p241.
80   J Winter and B Blaggett, op cit, p241.
81   Ibid, p233.
82   J Williams, op cit, p222.

83   Ibid, p127.
84   L James, *Mutiny* (Buchan and Enright, 1987), p78.
85   M Ferro, op cit, p198.
86   Ibid.
87   L James, op cit, p93.
88   M Ferro, op cit, p202.
89   Ibid, p202.
90   J Winter and B Blaggett, op cit, p278.
91   C Harman, *The Lost Revolution*, op cit, p28.
92   Ibid, p29.
93   T Cliff, op cit, p194.
94   Ibid, p202.
95   Quoted in M Ferro, op cit, p208.
96   Ibid, p211.
97   Ibid, p212.
98   Quoted in A Rothstein, op cit, p23.
99   M Ferro, op cit, p212.
100 A Rothstein, op cit, p35.
101 L James, op cit, p133.
102 Ibid, p134.
103 A Rothstein, op cit, p78.
104 L James, op cit, p153.
105 A Rothstein, op cit, p95.
106 Ibid, p100.
107 C Harman, *The Lost Revolution*, op cit, p30.
108 E J Leed, op cit, p198.
109 C Harman, *The Lost Revolution*, op cit, p44.
110 E J Leed, op cit, p189.
111 Ibid, p186.
112 Ibid.
113 C Bambery, 'Euro Fascism; the Lessons of the Past and Current Tasks', *International Socialism* 60, p9.
114 Ibid, p11.
115 A Rothstein, op cit, p68.
116 Ibid, p94.
117 Ibid.
118 C Rosenberg, *1919* (London, 1987), p7.
119 Ibid, p31.
120 Quoted in J Rees, op cit, p9.
121 Quoted in R C Nation, op cit, p5.
122 Quoted ibid, p35.
123 Quoted in T Cliff, op cit, p4.
124 Quoted in R C Nation, op cit, p36.
125 Quoted ibid, p37.
126 Quoted ibid, p55.
127 Quoted ibid, p45.
128 L Trotsky, *War and the International* (Wesley Press, 1971), p88.
129 Ibid, p218.
130- Quoted in R C Nation, op cit, p83.
131 Ibid, p216.
132 Quoted ibid, p138.
133 Ibid, p155.
134 Quoted ibid, p164.
135 Ibid.

136   V I Lenin, *The April Theses* (Moscow, 1985), p34.

137   Ibid.

138   Lenin's theory comes under frequent attack, however, from academics as well as from left wingers of various stripes—for example, S F Kissin, in his book *War and the Marxists*, argues that revolutionary defeatism cannot apply outside the very specific circumstances of Russia in the First World War. He sees Lenin's theory as 'ambiguous'—how can socialists wish for the defeat of their own country without wishing for the victory of others?

        Kissin argues that only defeated nations experience revolutions after war. This is used as a justification for his support for defencism—since there cannot be a successful revolution in a victorious nation, and since there must be a victor, therefore international revolution is not possible and one may as well support ones own ruling class, especially against the territorial advances of another. He sees revolutionary defeatism as a political slogan that was limited in time and space, a 'purely Russian phenomenon'. In the case of Germany, he sees the long term results of defeat in war as leading to a 'colossal reverse of socialism' in the rise of the Nazis, refuting the 'Leninist expectation that defeat would produce proletarian revolution and socialism.' This is misleading: the defeat of Germany in the war did contribute to the German Revolution, but Lenin never argued that socialism was inevitable. It was the defeat of the German *Revolution* that holds the key in the subsequent history of Germany and the world. The theory of revolutionary defeatism cannot be held responsible for such a calamity.

        Kissin has trouble with Lenin's theory not because it is not a clear revolutionary position, but because his own beliefs about the Second World War as a just war, in which Russia should be defended, forces him to reject it. It is not Lenin who was inconsistent, but those who subsequently wish to justify Stalinism and accept capitalism on its own terms.

139   Quoted in R C Nation, op cit, p167.

A light in the darkness

A review of Morgan Philips Price, **Dispatches from the Revolution:
Russia 1916-18** *(Pluto Press, 1997) £8.99*

JUDY COX

When revolution swept Russia in 1917, several foreign journalists were
there to give inspiring accounts of it. Among these accounts, this volume
of writings by Morgan Philips Price deserves a special place. Unlike
many others, such as Victor Serge and John Reed, the Harrow and
Cambridge educated Price was not a socialist when he went to Russia.
His testimony as to the nature of the revolution is perhaps even more
valuable than theirs: he did not report as he did because he was sympathetic to the Bolsheviks; he became a Bolshevik sympathiser because of
what he saw and reported. As Eric Hobsbawm says in his brief foreword,
the book is not just a history of the Russian Revolution, it is 'a useful
corrective to the post-Soviet reaction to it.'[1]

Like Arthur Ransome, Price defended the Russian Revolution from
the propaganda of hostile governments. Yet while Ransome only wanted
'to see fair play' done by the Russian government, Price decided to 'sink
or swim with the soviets', and indeed the more he saw of the revolution,
the more he committed himself to it, risking hardship, near starvation
and the wrath of the British political establishment.[2] Shortly after the
October Revolution he wrote of the miserable physical conditions in
Russia, but added:

> *We are all compelled to provide one warm shirt and jacket for the revolu-
> tionary troops as a requisition without payment! We have got the dictatorship
> of the proletariat with a vengeance this time! But I rub my hands and chuckle*

with glee. May the day soon come when the proletariat of Western Europe does the same.[3]

Many of the articles collected here, some written for the *Manchester Guardian* and some personal letters, are published for the first time. They give a perspective on the revolution which is unique in two ways. Firstly, Price travelled very widely in Russia, from Georgia and the Volga, to Turkestan and central Asia, and was able to give an unforgettable picture of the diversity of the revolution. Secondly, Price was a fly on the wall at crucial debates and had a brilliant ability to grasp changes in the consciousness of the masses. His writings are full of what he called the 'only true voice of Russia', and give an authenitic flavour of the political debates that went on in every town and village across the country.

The furthest reaches of the revolution

After suffering years of bloody war and repression, Price, along with millions of others, celebrated the February Revolution and the Tsar's abdication. He wrote:

> [The] *whole country is wild with joy, waving red flags and singing* Marseillaise. *It has surpassed my wildest dreams and I can hardly believe it is true. After two and a half years of mental suffering and darkness I at last begin to see light.*[4]

Two days later, Price noted how deeply the revolution had penetrated the oppressed masses of Russia. He reported from a mass gathering of people from across the Caucasus, called to mark the end of the Tsar's reign. It was a meeting which gave a glimpse of how the hopes roused by the revolution could unite people across ancient ethnic and religious divides. Price was deeply moved by the transformation he witnessed:

> *Here had assembled almost every element in the multiracial population of this part of the empire. There were wild mountain tribes, Lesgians, Avars, Chechens and Swanetians in their long black cloaks and sheepskin caps. In the recesses of the Caucasus range, where their homes lie, the eddies of the waves of revolution had swept... For years they have been sunk in apathy, fatalism and scepticism, and their racial feuds have been purposely fomented by the old government. Now the flood of their combined intellect and energy had burst forth and broken the rotten banks of privilege and oppression. I felt as I looked on that crowd that I was in the presence of a great physical phenomenon. The spirit of Demos had suddenly risen out of a multitude of suppressed personalities, and had appeared in the form of the great con-*

course of medieval mountaineers and 20th century proletariat, all inspired by one idea—brotherhood and freedom.[5]

In the late summer and autumn of 1917, after a visit to Petrograd, Price was off on his travels again. What he reported in those few months is very important for socialists seeking to defend the legacy of the Russian Revolution. Contrary to the long standing academic fashion for acknowledging that the February Revolution was a legitimate, spontaneous revolution, but then arguing that the October Revolution was a Bolshevik-inspired coup, lacking majority support, Price notes how life in rural Russia during these months was dominated by two great, and at times competing, tendencies. The first was desperation, starvation, and utter war weariness, all resulting from the failure of the post-February Provisional government to bring peace or redistribute land to the peasantry.

The second tendency was a growing spirit of hope and solidarity generated by the revolution which was deepening and spreading to the remotest areas of Russia. Price's stories demonstrate how the movement for change continued to intensify among the masses long after February. In Samara, for example, Price met some most unlikely rebels:

The revolution had penetrated into the sacred precincts of the monastery; the monks had gone on strike and had turned out the abbot, who had gone off whining to the Holy Synod... On enquiry into the ideas entertained by the monks for developing their little revolution, I found that they had already entered into an arrangement with the local peasantry. They were to keep enough land for themselves to work, and the rest was to go into the local commune.[6]

Price has a brilliant eye for the kind of details which demonstrate how profoundly the revolution touched every area of life. Visiting the Volga River, he noted the changes among the Muslim Tartar women. He points out that the women's movement started after the 1905 Revolution, which led to women abandoning their veils. After the February Revolution, the women elected their own delegates to the first All-Russian Muslim Conference, where they passed a motion condemning polygamy and inheritance laws. To Price it appears that the 'Muslim women are socially the equals of men and have at last shaken off from themselves the shackles of sex tyranny'.[7]

October: how the Bolsheviks gained ascendency

Price's account of Russia provides more than inspiring examples of the potential of revolution to overcome oppression. His sharp observations of key figures and events in the revolution, and the dynamics of the revolutionary process itself, flatly contradict right wing interpretations of the Russian Revolution. First, Price sheds light on the demise of the Provisional government, which some historians claim was the legitimate government of Russia, overthrown by the unrepresentative Bolsheviks. The Provisional government was dominated by the bourgeois Cadet Party and supported by the Petrograd Soviet, on the understanding that both shared a policy that peace should be made on the basis of no annexations and of respecting the rights of nations to self determination. But when Price interviewed the Provisional government's minister of foreign affairs, the Cadet Miliukov, he insisted that Russia would not accept peace unless it was granted the annexation of Constantinople, which meant the hated war dragging on. When the content of Price's interview became known there was a tremendous outcry, with demonstrations and riots against the war. Price recognised that far from having broad-based support, 'The bourgeois Provisional government, left high and dry, had nothing to rest upon. The old regime was gone; the vast masses of workers, soldiers and peasants had no confidence in them and were organising themselves and working out their own programmes'.[8]

Miliukov was forced to resign, but the government itself was saved by the Mensheviks and Socialist Revolutionaries (SRs) who agreed to enter into a coalition with the Cadets. The Mensheviks and SRs argued that because Russia was so undeveloped it would only be possible to have a bourgeois revolution. On that basis, they sought to compromise with the bourgeoisie to limit the scope of the revolution. At first Price had some sympathy with the Mensheviks and SRs. He showed great admiration for Kerensky, a Socialist Revolutionary who became president of the Provisional government, and approved of his tactics: 'Seeing the danger of a full proletariat revolution in an economically undeveloped and unorganised country, they had stood for a policy of temporary conciliation between the masses and the capitalists.'

During the next few months, however, it became increasingly obvious to everyone that such a compromise was unacceptable both to the masses, who nearly made an insurrection in July, and to the capitalists, who supported General Kornilov's attempt to overthrow the government. Price did not witness these events at first hand because he was touring Russia, but he grasped the shift in consciousness that Kornilov's attempted coup generated among the workers and peasants. The Kornilov coup exposed both the right wing's plans to overthrow the revolution, and exposed Kerensky, who was 'either unwilling or unable to stand courageously against these counter-revolutionary plots'. Price realised that the attempted military coup undermined all the Provisional government's efforts at effecting a compromise between the bourgeoisie and the working classes. He wrote, 'The masses in the country won't endure a coalition government which betrays the revolution behind their backs any longer.' He also noted how support was shifting quickly in favour of the Bolsheviks who had proved that they could defend the revolution: 'Lack of confidence in the Provisional government is everywhere expressed even among the moderate members of the revolutionary democracy. The councils are becoming more and more Maximalist [Bolshevik] in their composition. Since the Kornilov rebellion they have demanded that all power should go into their hands...'[9]

Price explains how it was that the polarisation in Russian society undermined the Provisional government, not Bolshevik plots. The Mensheviks and SRs in the Provisional government espoused the politics of compromise and were therefore doomed to vacillate and dither while those they sought to reconcile grew further and further apart. In an article printed on 20 November 1917, he explained how the second Provisional government, involving the Mensheviks and SRs, fell because it stood between two increasingly divided class and could meet the aspirations of the neither:

> The government of M Kerensky fell before the Bolsheviks insurgents because it had no supporters in the country. The bourgeois parties and the generals of the Staff dislike it because it would not establish a military dictatorship. The revolutionary democracy lost faith in it because after eight months it had neither given land to the peasants nor established state control of industries nor advanced the cause of the Russian peace programme... The Bolsheviks acquired great support all over the country. In my journey in the provinces in September and October I noticed that every local soviet had been captured by them.[10]

It is equally mistaken to think that the October Revolution involved only a small number of workers capturing a few military positions and nothing more. In chapter six of *Dispatches*, which is taken from his *Reminiscences of the Russian Revolution*, Price gives a memorable account of the days of the October Revolution. He shows the paralysis and depression of the Mensheviks and the contrastingly resolute plans executed by the Bolsheviks. He gives a sense of the atmosphere, the rumours of counter-revolutionary plots, the debates at the Second Soviet Congress and the first long-awaited decrees granting land to the peasants, control of industry to the workers and the immediate armistice. Price's experiences reveal time and time again that this was above all a revolution from below, a revolution carried through by the majority, not through the military prowess or duplicity of a minority. He recalled:

It was already clear to me that the Bolshevik Military Revolutionary Committee was not in control of an army in the ordinary sense of the word. The Red Guard detachments were very largely independent of one another, electing their own commanders and removing them whenever the rank and file saw fit... Hunger and hatred of wage slavery alone bound them together with a band of iron.[11]

Nor was the revolutionary activity limited to the great metropolitan centres. Price writes of how, in the first few days after the October Revolution, news trickled in to Petrograd from the length and breadth of the great Russian plain. Far from being aloof from the insurrection, Price discovered that in some areas of central Russia local soviets anticipated events in Petrograd. He concluded that what the Bolsheviks did in Petrograd was only a reflection of similar actions taking place in different forms and situations across Russia.

Contemporary commentators frequently criticise the Bolsheviks for weakening support for the revolution by attempting to rule without the other working class parties. This argument was raised in the days immediately following the revolution, when few thought the Soviet government could survive. Price recalls meeting a Menshevik in the street:

'The Bolsheviks have made a great mistake in seizing power by these methods,' he said, 'They cannot possibly hold it unless the moderate democratic parties come to their aid.' This view of a Russian progressive intellectual was very similar to those of outside observers at this time... On the following day, however, there was a different feeling in the air. It seemed as if there was, for the first time for many months, a political force in the country that knew what it wanted. This was clearly reflected in the common talk in the streets. Outside the Circus Modern a large crowd had assembled for a meeting at which delegates from the Soviet Congress were going to speak... No word was said about the violent methods by which the Bolsheviks had come into power. The deeds which shocked the tender feelings of the intellectual did not trouble the realist politician of the street. Would they be able to bring food to the towns and bring an end to the war? That was the question being asked. The Tsar's government could not do it, nor could Kerensky's. 'Give these people a chance,' were the words I heard coming from all sides...[12]

This account of the political atmosphere in Petrograd during the October Revolution shows how the failure of alternatives based on compromise and parliamentary institutions led to people choosing the Bolsheviks, as opposed to the Bolsheviks eliminating all possible alternatives. Neither did the Bolsheviks choose their isolation. The Bolsheviks did join a coalition with Left SRs, until the Left SRs resorted to terrorism to try and block the Brest-Litovsk treaty. Price points out that this was much regretted by the Bolsheviks: 'Now the Bolsheviks are quite alone, and upon them rests the superhuman task of bearing the cross of the revolution against the armed camps of Europe until the democracies of other lands awake'.[13]

Running through Price's anecdotes and descriptions is a growing awareness that the deep polarisation in Russian society created a crisis which the old political institutions were incapable of resolving. He briefly develops this point in relation to the Bolsheviks' controversial disbanding of the long-awaited Constituent Assembly. While Price is dubious about some of the Bolsheviks's tactics, he does explain that the deep class divisions would inevitably undermine the authority of the Constituent Assembly, which would, 'reflect these bitter divisions in a concentrated form'. In addition, Price gives further evidence of the point made before in *International Socialism*, namely that the Constituent Assembly had no popular support among the majority of Russian society who knew that the soviets were far more effective.[14] Price notes, 'The soldiers, sailors, and workers regard their syndicates or soviets as the sole authority which they will respect'.[15]

Finally, Price is very interesting in his assessment of the role Lenin and the Bolsheviks played during the revolution. Initially Price, like many since, thought them fanatical demagogues, and reported their growing support only grudgingly. In the autumn of 1917 he noted, 'The Maximalist fanatics, who still dream of the social revolution throughout all Europe, have, according to my observations in the provinces, recently acquired an immense, if amorphous following'.[16] Yet within months, Price had a glimpse of the power of the Soviet government to solve problems, to create new methods of organising new institutions, as well as overthrowing the old ones. His growing recognition of the role that the Bolsheviks played was strengthened when Lenin supported signing the Brest-Litovsk peace treaty despite its punitive terms, in a desperate attempt to buy time for rebuilding Russia. Price recognised that Lenin could take responsibility for hard decisions if the future of the revolution was at stake.

Price asserted time and time again that the hardship and near starvation experienced by the Russians was a result of the savagery of the Allied blockade and the disruption of the civil war, not the policies of the Soviet government. He became so involved in the revolution that he was employed by the Soviet government to produce a revolutionary paper in English, *The Call*. His first job was to translate an appeal by Lenin to Allied troops landing in Russia, to be distributed by aeroplane. By July 1918 Price had decided that Lenin was the 'most courageous statesman in Europe at present and history will, I believe, put him as one of the greatest brains of the period'.[17]

This book is a brilliant supplement to other histories of the Russian Revolution. It illustrates the experiences of revolution, which transformed Morgan Philips Price the English country gentleman, into Morgan Philips Price the passionate advocate of the socialist revolution. When he left Russia, he went with the approval of the Soviet government to report on the focus of Russia's hopes, the German Revolution. Price joined the British Communist Party in 1922, but became disillusioned with the policies of the Comintern and left in 1924. Although Price eventually became a Labour MP, he never repudiated the experiences that had so moved him as a young man—he never lost sight of the significance of the Russian Revolution and the great hopes for peace and liberation that it inspired. A few weeks before his death in 1973 he wrote, 'Naturally I see things more in perspective today but I do not in the least belittle what I saw and wrote then. I still regard the Russian Revolution as the most important thing that had happened at that period of time'.[18]

Notes
1   M Philips Price, *Dispatches from the Revolution: Russia 1916-18* (Pluto Press, 1917), pxii.
2   The hardship was very real. A visiting journalist who met Price in 1917 described him as 'emaciated'. Price's reports were heavily censored by the British establishment, firstly because they were critical of conditions and anti-Semitism in Tsarist Russia, and later because they were so critical of Allied intervention. He was threatened with arrest under the Defence of the Realm Act several times and was actually imprisoned for a few days in Germany.
3   M Philips Price, op cit, p110.
4   Ibid, p30.
5   Ibid, pp31-32.
6   Ibid, p61.
7   Ibid, p74.
8   Ibid, p44.
9   Ibid, p55.
10   Ibid, p88.
11   Ibid, p97-98.
12   Ibid, p94.
13   Ibid, p136.
14   See J Rees, 'In Defence of October', *International Socialism* 52, p24. Now reprinted in book form (Bookmarks, 1997).
15   M Philips Price, op cit, p107.
16   Ibid, p108.
17   Ibid, p137.
18   Ibid, p155.

Victor Serge: writing for the future

*A review of Victor Serge, **Russia Twenty Years After** (Humanities Press, 1996), £13.50*

PETE GLATTER

Russia Twenty Years After was one of the very few books of the 1930s which was clear about the counter-revolutionary nature of Stalinism at the time. It tells the messy truth about Russia at the time of industrialisation. And in doing so, it comes surprisingly close to telling us about the nature of Russia today. In order to appreciate the quality of Victor Serge's achievement, it is worth looking briefly at the circumstances in which he wrote this book. The rise of Stalin to the position of dictator over the Soviet Union was no ordinary defeat for the revolutionary left. There had been defeats before but the left had survived and regrouped. After the Russian revolution of 1905 had been defeated, for example, Lenin remarked that a beaten army learns its lessons well. This was entirely accurate: despite vicious repression, the Russian workers took power within little more than a decade. The coming of Stalin was more like Armageddon. Of the purges which followed, the first and most comprehensive was directed against the Left Opposition within the Communist Party of the Soviet Union (CPSU). Serge quotes at length from one of the many Trotskyists who took part in the resistance to this political genocide:

> *On 22 January, 1931, the anniversary of Lenin's death, all the deported Bolshevik-Leninists of Akmolinsk [Kazakhstan] were arrested and incarcerated in cells infected with typhoid. There were 12 of us, including two women; nine contracted typhoid...*

> *In the Verkhne-Uralsk prison the Bolshevik-Leninists, to the number of 450, began a hunger strike to protest against the despotism of the local administration. The year before, in the course of a hunger strike, the director Biziukov gave the order to douse our comrades with cold water—this in winter and in Siberia! The order was executed. When our comrades began to barricade the cells, the jailers directed the water hose into their eyes. Our comrade Pogossian lost his sight. In 1931, a turnkey fired a shot through a grille into the chest of comrade Essayan. On the days of revolutionary festivals, we had serious conflicts with the administration. We were either incarcerated or beaten up because we sang the 'International.'*
>
> *In the Petropavlovsk prison I saw 35 women, eight of them with nursing babies, shut up in a cell of 25 square metres. The only access to air was through the peephole. I shall never forget those piteous and puny children! Taking turns, the mothers held them up to the peephole so that they might breathe a wretched ration of fresh air...*
>
> *We began our hunger strike* [in Verkhne-Uralsk, against the automatic doubling of sentences] *on 11 December, 1933... They began to feed us forcibly. Unspeakable violence was the result, the voluntarily famished men battling with the jailers. Our comrades, of course, were trounced. At the end of our strength, they crammed rubber hose down our mouths and throats. The famished men were dragged to the 'feeding cell' like so many dogs. Nobody gave in. On the fifteenth day we decided to suspend the strike because the attempts at suicide were becoming too numerous...*[1]

So complete was the destruction that when Russia emerged from the collapse of the Soviet Union in 1991, it contained no organised left of any kind. Stalinist terror obliterated revolutionary socialism in Russia for over 60 years. The same could not be said about other targets of repression: nationalism among the non-Russian peoples of the USSR, the Russian Orthodox Church, the dissident movement of the 1970s—let alone the more tolerated nationalist and monarchist groupings among the Russians themselves.

Trotsky and Victor Serge were prominent among the handful of voices in the 1930s which spoke out insistently against Stalinism without abandoning their socialist principles. But few listened to them. The left throughout the world had already been carved up between Stalinism and social democracy (Labourism, in its British incarnation). Accusations made by the Stalinised Communist parties that Trotskyites were in league with the fascists struck a chord with those for whom the Soviet Union seemed to be the great bulwark against Nazi barbarism. It was in Russia that the armies of fascism were decisively beaten. Stalin and the Red Army were publicly glorified by the left and by right wing leaders like Churchill.

In such circumstances, denunciations of Soviet bureaucracy were likely to get a hostile reception. Revolutionaries like Trotsky and Serge made their stand in the most difficult conditions. Trotsky was murdered. Serge effectively died of hunger a few years later. If they made mistakes, the wonder is that they did not make many more. Trotsky more than anyone kept alive a tradition of revolutionary socialism which was independent of either Stalinism or social democracy. It was a tremendous achievement.

One of the most pernicious aspects of Stalinism was its ability to incorporate former revolutionaries and use their talents in the industrialisation drive before executing them as scapegoats. There is always a pressure on the defeated to accommodate to the victors. The greater the scale of the defeat, the greater the temptation to compromise. Stalinism had the additional advantage of appearing to offer the only way forward for the USSR through industrialisation and the collectivisation of agriculture (in reality, the smashing of the peasantry). A most painful and revealing passage in the postscript to *Russia Twenty Years After* is the one in which Serge describes the reaction to it of those *closest* to him:

> *I put the finishing touches to this book in January 1937. Many of my best friends hesitated to approve its publication. Their attachment to the revolution impelled them to ask if I was not drawing too black a picture of the Soviet Union of today; if the involuntary or even unconscious resentment of an outlaw was not playing some part in the book.*

Serge's response to this is a model of revolutionary courage in the face of adversity:

> *The past year shows that all the oppositions which, in the last 14 years, stood up against the bureaucratic regime, underrated its profoundly counter-revolutionary power and, still more, its inhumanity. The judgments formulated hitherto by the Left Opposition to which I belonged, sinned only in indulgence and optimism, because the Opposition stuck to preserving at all costs the last chances, however feeble, of a political redressment, of a great reform which would have brought the Soviet Union back to the road of socialism.*[2]

It was necessary for revolutionaries to tell the truth about Stalinism. But it was excruciatingly hard to do so. Most of the people with revolutionary aspirations, and there were millions of them, believed the lie. They wanted to believe it. They needed to believe. Their illusions about Stalinism and about the Soviet Union were the product of the most terrible defeats: the defeat of the German Revolution, of the Hungarian Revolution, of the Italian *Biennio Rosso*, of the British General Strike, of the Chinese Revolution a year later and finally of the Spanish Revolution in the civil war. As Victor Serge shows in this book, Stalinism both grew out of these defeats and contributed to them. The more workers were defeated, the more people's hopes of bringing about change by their own efforts were dashed. The more these hopes were dashed, the more they pinned their faith on the red star of the Soviet Union, shining bravely in the deepening gloom. The illusions bred by defeat are always about some agency other than the working class holding the key to the future. Of all such illusions, Stalinism has been the greatest and the most destructive.

Counter-revolution in Russia

One of the themes to which Serge returns again and again is how alien the early Soviet regime was to the bureaucratic tyranny which replaced it. In October 1917 the Bolsheviks had led a revolution based on the rank and file democracy of the workers' and soldiers' Soviets (councils). They had overthrown the unelected Provisional Government, taken Russia out of the First World War, decreed workers' control over production and given the land to the peasants. The superpowers of the day—Britain, the USA and their allies—made a prolonged attempt to destroy the new regime, already beset by famine and industrial collapse. They invaded Russia, inspired a ruinous civil war and imposed an economic blockade. The civil war period left a terrible mark on the revolutionary regime. Its human foundation was destroyed: the workers of 1917 perished either in battle or through famine, or they disappeared into the countryside. Soviet democracy gave way to militarisation and then to the one-party state. It was a desperate situation, which dictated what Serge rightly calls 'measures of public safety, sometimes terrible ones'. This 'dictatorship of the proletariat' may have deprived the anarchists and the more right wing socialists, such as the Mensheviks and the Socialist Revolutionaries, of 'the right to sabotage, even with the best of intentions'. But such doubtful allies of the Soviet regime, not to speak of dissidents within the ruling party (now renamed as the Communist Party), continued to publish their views quite openly. Only in 1927, the year in which the Trotskyists were expelled, could Stalin's henchmen proclaim that under the dictatorship of the proletariat there could be a number of parties: one in power, the rest in prison.

> In theory and in practice, the prison-state has nothing in common with the measures of public safety of the commune-state in the period of battles: it is the work of the triumphant bureaucrats, who, in order to impose their usurpation, are forced to break with the essential principles of socialism and to refuse the workers any freedom at all.[3]

Everywhere Serge looked, he found the same rupture, both in spirit and in practice. Under the slogan of 'Socialism in one country,' the top priority of Soviet foreign policy changed, not without the odd zigzag, from spreading the revolution to cultivating the sympathies of other upper classes. Stalin delivered the Chinese Revolution into the hands of the executioners of the nationalist Kuomintang so as 'not to frighten either the Chinese bourgeoisie or the powers'.[4] A brief lurch to the ultra-left had the German Communist Party refusing to unite with the Social Democratic Party against the Nazis, thus allowing Hitler into power. This disaster, though unacknowledged, frightened the Stalinists into a revamped version of their previous tactic. Known as the 'Popular Front against Fascism', it was an attempt to submerge the class struggle in an all-class alliance, in the forlorn hope of surrounding Germany with defence treaties which meant something. Even fascist Italy was apparently considered to be a potential ally:

> *In the August 1936 number of **Lo Stato Operaio**, official organ of the Italian Communist Party, we find an appeal for the reconciliation of all Italians, from which we quote the following remarkable lines:*
> *'Italian people! Fascists of the Old Guard! Young fascists! We communists adopt as our own the fascist programme of 1919 which is a programme of peace, of freedom, of defence of the interests of the workers, and we say to you: Let us fight unitedly to realise this programme!'* [5]

In Spain, where republicans were fighting a civil war against the fascists, Serge predicted that the Stalinist bureaucracy was intervening 'in order to prepare there the repression of the revolutionary tendencies that combat it and to profit by the aid it lends the republic in order to assure its own political hegemony within it'.[6] This is the theme of Ken Loach's film *Land and Freedom*. Serge need only have added that the Stalinists achieved this aim at the cost of demoralisation, soon followed by defeat. But what of the situation inside Russia?

Serge lived in the Soviet Union for 17 years, from 1919 to 1936. He had been a machine-gunner in the civil war and had then worked closely with the Bolshevik leadership. Expelled from the CPSU as an oppositionist in 1928 (and briefly held under arrest), he managed to stay clear of the authorities for a further five years, during which he travelled around the USSR and lived for a time in the countryside. In 1933 he was arrested, held in solitary confinement and interrogated before being to deported to Orenburg, where he and his son nearly died of hunger, and here he remained until his expulsion from the Soviet Union in 1936. Serge's testimony is therefore that of an eyewitness and a participant, someone who can communicate the feel and the smell of Russian life in

Stalin's heyday. He does this with incomparable skill. Two passages in particular stand out from the many which detail more dramatic instances of brutality and injustice. Both are about the struggle and drudgery of everyday life. The first gives the more general picture:

> *In order to get an idea of the life of the Soviet citizen during these years one must picture the worker preoccupied with obtaining, stamping, checking, and re-registering a bread card, which is refused to half the workers on various pretexts; the housewife, running from one empty store to another, and registering in a queue at the doors of a fishstall early in the evening, pauper No 758, in order to wrangle the next morning over a ration of salt fish; the worker exposed to spying in the shop, coming home to comment at the table on the arrests made the night before; finding rhymed apologies for the death penalty in his paper; not knowing where he can get a spare shirt; fearing to be driven out of the big city by being refused a passport, because his son has married the daughter of a former small merchant; wondering what risky combination to resort to in order to get hold of a dollar and buy some precious medicament at the Torgsin* [the State Society for Trading with Foreigners]... *Hemmed in by the police, by poverty, by lies.*[7]

The second passage is specifically about women. But since it depicts them in terms of class, it is symbolic of human, social relationships in the USSR as a whole:

> *The social differentiation obliges us to distinguish the various conditions of Soviet women. The upper strata of society, especially numerous in the centres, have produced the type of elegant and indolent lady, who follows the fashions, the theatre, the concerts, who is desolated when she is unable to get the latest dance records from abroad, who tans herself every year on the beaches of the Crimea or the Caucasus. I have heard the elegant in the literary salons praising the enthusiasm of the Donietz miners and the political wisdom of the Leader. I have seen others, fat and dressed in transparent silks, leaning on the arms of aviation officers, walking past children with bellies swollen from famine who moaned softly as they lay stretched out in the dust. Flies resting on their eyelids and lips tormented them. The ladies turned their heads away. After all, they were only little Kazaks or Kirghiz...*
>
> *Below this feminine aristocracy is the average housewife of modest means, as needy as she is everywhere else. Still lower—and she constitutes the majority—is the woman of the people, a worker or peasant, who does the washing, goes for water to the fountain or to the river (in winter, it is to a hole punctured in the ice), takes care of the animals, raises the children, receives the drunken man at the end of the week, stands in line in front of the stores, buys a few metres of satinette in order to resell them and, thanks to this bril-*

liant stroke of business, is able to provide shoes for the youngest. The foreign litterateurs do not come to question her while travelling. Disfigured and aged at thirty-five, she sometimes takes to drink. Then you hear her—on the revolutionary holidays—singing in a discordant voice the old popular plaints.[8]

If there is any doubt about the state in which the workers undertook the immense labour of industrialisation, one only has to know that in Omsk, a major Russian city and the capital of western Siberia, the first proper sewers were not built until 1939.[9] This kind of thing was not primarily to do with backwardness but with priorities. The regime which was demanding unheard of sacrifices from its workers was as unsympathetic to them as elegant Soviet ladies were to starving children. The workers and peasants who slaved to construct Soviet industry were the victims of low pay, shortages, absolute police power, famine and disease. Contrary to official propaganda, the welfare state had been all but destroyed and there was even a Soviet version of prescription charges.[10] The restoration of ranks in the Soviet army in 1935 followed the revival of privilege throughout Soviet society. Pay could vary from 70 rubles a month for a woman worker through 1,000 to 10,000 rubles for high communist functionaries and specialists to millions for the painters, poets and novelists who danced attendance on the top leadership. But these differentials were greatly magnified by other forms of privilege:

...the collaborator of a scientific institute gets only 300 to 400 rubles, but he works in two or three institutes, which comes to 1,200 rubles at the end of the month. The newspaper editor, at 250 rubles a month, collaborates on other publications, which trebles his income. The factory director, at 500 or 1,500 rubles, gets himself granted premiums for the execution of plans on the occasion of festivals and anniversaries. The party functionaries and the communist leaders receive gifts of garments made of fine cloth, are lodged by the party in comfortable quarters built for that purpose, have the benefits of watering places in the Caucasus or the Crimea, free of charge or at reduced rates...

Every category of workers, every factory—and within each factory the ordinary workers, the shock workers, the technical men, the bureaucrats—has its private store, closed to other categories, with special rations and prices, confidential or secret. No displays, just a card that is open-sesame. As a rule, the reserved stores of the foreigners, the high functionaries, the GPU [the secret police], the well-paid specialists, are sufficiently supplied with merchandise. Those of the ordinary workers and of the population at large are dirty and virtually empty. The government intervenes in order to fix the minimum rations of the workers and fixes them at a level appreciably below requirements... I saw this placard in a bureau: 'Grandparents have no right to food cards'...[11]

The leadership which boasted about having achieved socialism (in 1934!) reversed the great reforms made by the first Soviet government. The right to free abortion, 'a capital conquest of the revolution,' was replaced by abortion as a crime in all but the narrowest medical circumstances. Other legal measures restricted divorce through penal taxation, effectively fining couples who wished to separate. New laws re-criminalised homosexuality and pornography—and there was no mucking about with unnecessary details like defining what pornography was. Capital punishment was restored, introduced as a punishment for theft and extended, along with other penalties, to children of 12 (according to Stalinist educationalists, this was justified by the high quality of Soviet education, which turned children into adults by the age of 12—not, as Serge remarks, that they were allowed to vote or stand in elections, of course). Soviet criminal law had initially been the most advanced in the world, confining itself to defending society rather than punishing or avenging. Now it was no better than fascist law.[12] For such achievements, there was a constant and deafening chorus of praise and approval. The 1936 constitution, for example, was compared to Beethoven's Ninth Symphony.[13] But this was small beer next to the carefully manufactured and orchestrated leadership cult, for which worship is not too strong a word:

> **Pravda** *of 28 August, 1936, publishes the translation of an Uzbek poem which attributes to the Leader the creation of the world:*
>
> *O great Stalin, O leader of the peoples,*
> *Thou who broughtest man to birth,*
> *Thou who fructifiest the earth…*
> *Thou who makest bloom the spring,*
> *Thou who makest vibrate the musical cords.*
> *Thou, splendour of my spring, O Thou,*
> *Sun reflected by millions of hearts…*

There was no doubt in Serge's mind that the changes of the Stalin era were profoundly reactionary. But, like Trotsky, he was not sure how far the process of reaction had gone. So on the one hand, he describes the Stalinist bureaucracy, in some detail, as counter-revolutionary, and on the other he argues that nationalisation and planning are for the Russian workers the surviving victories of the revolution. 'It has proved possible to rob them of the fruits of these victories,' he adds, almost in the same breath.[15] In *Alice in Wonderland*, the Cheshire Cat disappears but his smile remains behind. Serge's argument sounds rather similar. If the workers had been robbed of the fruits of their victories, then *nothing* remained of them apart from the memory—and nationalisation and planning were not necessarily incompatible with counter-revolution. The Russian Revolution is, as Serge says, 'a historical experience of incalculable scope', and it is partly thanks to him that an non-Stalinised memory of it has been kept alive. But memory is not the same as victory. The idea that from the victories represented by nationalisation and planning Russian workers would derive the confidence to rise up against their Stalinist masters (for this is what Serge was arguing) was profoundly misleading and was bound to lead to demoralisation. The truth was that the common people of the USSR had been bled white by civil war and isolation. They hardly had time to recover before the Stalinist dictatorship butchered a large minority and turned the rest into factory fodder. There was no prospect here of a revolutionary struggle for power in anything but the long term.

The disappointment of Serge's own expectations seems evident in his 1947 article, 'Thirty Years After the Russian Revolution,' also printed here. Stalinism was by now extending its grip from one state to eight— strengthening its hold throughout Eastern Europe and, in a different form, preparing for power in China. Yet Serge was, if anything, further away from an understanding of what had happened. His defence of the Russian Revolution is all the weaker for two accusations he makes against the Bolshevik Party.[16]

The first is that the creation of the Cheka (the Extraordinary Commission for the Repression of Counter-Revolution) was the 'most incomprehensible error' of the Bolsheviks, and one which led directly to Stalin's secret police, the GPU. The Cheka was not an exclusively Bolshevik creation: supporters of the revolution set up local Chekas for the internal defence of the revolution just as they responded to the call for a Red Army for external defence. The Cheka was a cruel necessity of the civil war, especially at the height of the White offensive in 1919, when the Soviet republic resembled a beleaguered fortress in an area occupying 600 kilometres around Moscow. There were misgivings in the Bolshevik leadership about the growth in the Cheka's power and it was drastically reduced once the civil war was over.[17] Stalin had to more or less start from scratch when he developed the secret police into an instrument of control over all other institutions. Serge's second allegation is that the suppression of the Kronstadt revolt in 1921 was a panic overreaction—a prime example of the kind of mistake that was made once the Bolsheviks were in power. The basic facts of the matter were that the fortress of Kronstadt commanded the approaches to Petrograd (later Leningrad, now St Petersburg). Had such a breach been allowed to open up in the heart of Soviet territory, it would almost certainly have restarted the civil war. The suppression of Kronstadt was extremely brutal but it enabled the regime to survive for a few more years. These accusations (criticisms seems too mild a word) let the great imperialist powers, whose pressure distorted the young Soviet regime, off the hook. They suggest by default that a socialist regime could have flourished in Russia despite the failure of the revolution to spread if only it had been nicer. And they imply that Leninism did lead to Stalinism after all, despite all of Serge's protestations to the contrary.

In Serge's defence, it must be said that—in addition to his worsening physical condition—the situation was less clear to him than it is with the benefit of hindsight. He sensed that there had been a change in the nature of the regime. We know it. We know that society and production were knocked into a completely different shape. We know that this was the greatest change ever to have taken place in Russia and the other components of the USSR. Even a typically conservative history of the Soviet Union describes it as 'The Great Rupture'.[18] We know that the secret police with Stalin as its real head replaced the Communist Party, bureaucratised and Stalinised though it was, as the key motivating element in the state machine. Huge bureaucratic ministries controlled every branch of the new industry (there were about 65 of them in the late 1980s). We know that all institutions of any importance were remade and purged over and over again until their leaderships were entirely new, cut off from the past. About 60 percent of the active communists of 1931 had been purged by 1937. Of the 139 members of the CPSU Central Committee elected at the Seventeenth Congress in 1934, 110 (79 percent) were arrested before the Eighteenth Congress in 1939. Of the 1,966 delegates who attended the Seventeenth Congress, only 59 turned up at the Eighteenth Congress: 1,108 (56 percent) had been arrested. The purges led to the wholesale destruction of the industrial managers who had led the first phase of industrialisation. Studies in the mid-1930s showed that only 3 to 8 percent of directors had held the same post for over five years. In 1937-1938, on the eve of the Second World War, Stalin removed more than 75 percent of the officer corps and the high command of the Red Army. We know that the forced labour population was probably around 8 to 9 million and that something in the region of 20 million people died through forced labour, collectivisation and the purges.[19]

It is not simply a matter of political changes, profound though these were. In a matter of ten years the industrialisation drive transformed Russian society and sent it off in a new direction. The official figures are not to be trusted, of course, but they give an idea of the scale of the change. Between 1913 and 1928, the signs are that not only did the USSR not develop, it actually went into reverse. The number of manual workers fell from 14.6 percent of the population to 12.4 percent. At the same time the proportion of peasants rose from 66.7 percent to 74.9 percent. Then it happened. Between 1928 and 1939 manual workers as a percentage of the population rose from 12.4 to 33.7. By 1959 the figure was 50.2 and by 1979 it was 60.0.[20] Then there is the question of the way the new economy was organised. Leonid Polezhaev, the present day governor of Omsk and for many years a leading communist in the economic management of the region, recently wrote: 'The Soviet economy—let's face the truth—was created for war and in the expectation of war.' He exemplifies this in terms of the extreme centralisation, the military organisation of the enterprises and their direct supervision by the state.[21] A leading western academic has put it like this:

> *Political competition with the West was now transformed into an economic race, but one whose standards and measures of achievement were set in the West... In the context of socialism in one country Stalinism was primarily a war machine, with the emphasis on heavy industry, a way of industrialising the country to sustain its military potential.*[22]

As Tony Cliff and others have argued, the subordination of the Soviet economy and society to the demands of military competition meant that the USSR had made the transition from the 'bureaucratically deformed workers' state' of the 1920s to state capitalism.[23] The position of the workers, their experience of the new order and their attitude towards it, was often best expressed in jokes like this one: Is it possible to build socialism in one country? It is. But its better to live in another country. [24]

Conclusion

The vivid, unforgettable impressions which crowd the pages of *Russia Twenty Years After* are its great strength and its weakness. Serge had some striking insights. He identified the discontent of the non-Russian nationalities as a threat to the regime 50 years before the USSR began to crack up along national lines. He understood that a regime of oppression which identified itself as the bearer of socialism had inspired a tremendous feeling of revulsion against socialism. The consequences of this are, of course, still with us. Nevertheless, this is not a work of analysis and Serge's account of Stalinism is not always systematic. He devotes two chapters to Stalin's foreign policy. But he mentions the rise to power of the Nazis in Germany only in passing, although this was a crucial event and one in which Stalinism had played a disastrous role.

On the other hand, Serge wrote this book very much as a companion volume to Trotsky's *The Revolution Betrayed*, which he was translating at the time. In this role, *Russia Twenty Years After* is a superb piece of work which Serge completed in an artistic sense with his magnificent novel *The Case of Comrade Tulayev*. *Russia Twenty Years After* begins with the condition of the workers and ends with the prospects for working class struggle. At the time those prospects were in fact minimal. The class struggle in Russia is now an established fact and the common use of phrases like 'fear of rising social tension' in Russia is a recognition of this. Serge may have been wrong to be over optimistic. But he was right not to give in to a defeat which seemed final, right to react against fatalism and despair. Out of the bitterness of unimaginable defeats, he transmitted a simple, shattering message of revolutionary hope: 'Nothing is ended, everything begins'.[25]

Notes

I would like to thank Mike Haynes for his help, his advice and for those of his manuscripts which, for some inexplicable reason, remain unpublished.

1   Victor Serge, *Russia Twenty Years After* (Humanties Press, 1996), pp 72-73.
2   Ibid, pp288-289.
3   Ibid, p93.
4   Ibid, p257.
5   Ibid, p269.
6   Ibid, p274.
7   Ibid, p184; in the richly furnished stores run by the Torgsin (the State Society for Trading with Foreigners) Soviet citizens could get good quality food, soap, shoes, cloth, medicine and other goods unobtainable anywhere else in exchange for hard currency and gold.
8   Ibid, pp25-26.
9   M P Zhuravlev, *Omsk: vchera, segodnya, zavtra* (Omsk, 1993), p69.
10   Victor Serge, *Russia Twenty Years After*, op cit, p6.
11   Ibid, pp5, 179-180.
12   Ibid, pp24-25, 186-190, 244.
13   Ibid, p206.
14   Ibid, pp131, 206.
15   Ibid, p287.
16   Ibid, pp309, 313.
17   See, for example, T Cliff, *Lenin*, Volume 3 (Bookmarks, 1987); J Rees, *In Defence of October* (London, 1997).
18   M Heller and A Nekrich, *Utopia in Power*, (London, 1986), p222.
19   R Sakwa, *Soviet Politics* (London, 1989), pp44-53; T Cliff, *Russia: a Marxist Analysis* (London, nd), p259.
20   Ibid, p48.
21   L Polezhaev, *Vpered, na medlennykh tormozakh...* (Moscow, 1994), p75.
22   R Sakwa, op cit, pp47, 59.
23   See, for example, T Cliff, op cit; P Binns, T Cliff, C Harman, *Russia: from Workers' State to State Capitalism* (London, 1987).
24   Iosif Raskin, *Entsiklopediye Khuliganstvuyshchego Ortodoksa* (St Petersburg, 1995), p380. I would like to thank Louis Loizou for providing me with this invaluable source of soviet humour.
25   Victor Serge, *Russia Twenty Years After*, op cit, p287.

A guide to action

A review of Paul Le Blanc, **From Marx to Gramsci** *(Humanities Press, 1996), £14.99*

GILL HUBBARD

The power of this book lies in Le Blanc's excellent selection and presentation of some of the most fundamental ideas of Marx, Engels, Lenin, Luxemburg, Trotsky and Gramsci. His choice of references and the framework for his selection rest on the premise that the central pivot of Marxism is 'proletarian revolutionary practice'. Despite Le Blanc's somewhat pessimistic assessment of the prospects for revolution it is worth stating that anyone who wishes to read the works of Marx, Engels, Lenin, Luxemburg, Trotsky and Gramsci in order to change the world, could not go far wrong with reading this book.

The book is divided into two parts. The first part is full of excellent quotations from the five selected Marxists, intertwined with Le Blanc's own intelligent analysis of their meaning. It is both informative and interesting. Le Blanc is, without doubt, someone who likes to debate with his readers rather than simply present the facts. The second part is devoted to excerpts from Marx and Engels, Lenin, Luxemburg, Trotsky and Gramsci. These have been carefully chosen for the reader as a guide to revolutionary practice. It is this aspect which makes the book so valuable.

The central pivot of Marxism

The writings of Marx, Engels, Lenin, Luxemburg, Trotsky and Gramsci are not only crucial for understanding the world and human history, they are also as, Lenin suggests, a 'guide to action'.[1] It is the practical political activity which brings the theory to life, and one without the other is useless. Le Blanc explains why the writings of these key Marxists were selected for a book which embraces Marxism as revolutionary practice. Despite differences in their outlook, Le Blanc argues that it 'is the underlying continuity of theoretical orientation and practical political perspective which unites them'.[2]

Le Blanc briefly explains in chapter one that Marx and Engels were influenced by German philosophy, classical political economy predominantly from Britain, and French political thought. But, as Le Blanc points out, it was the early working class radicalism which arose in Britain, France and Germany in the 1830s and 1840s which most profoundly shaped their distinctive ideas. It is worth quoting Le Blanc's own analysis of how *scientific socialism* (the term used by Marx and Engels to describe their body of thought) was developed:

> *The synthesis which Marx and Engels developed was not simply meant to advance human knowledge in the abstract. Despite the relatively fortunate circumstances in which they were born, they saw human misery all around them. The lives and labour of the many were consumed in providing for the wealth and comfort of powerful minorities; the mental, cultural and physical existence of mass labouring populations was degraded in the process. People suffered, and some died, under the innumerable assaults on their dignity and well-being, their potential for full human development stunted—all for the benefit of domineering and self-satisfied profiteers and rulers. Marx and Engels perceived this reality as being built into the social system of which they were part—not just the old order of aristocratic privilege, but also the rising order of bourgeois 'progress'.[3]*

The need to unite theory and practice lay at the heart of Marxism. Gramsci argued that there should be no separation or compartmentalisation of theory and practice in a revolutionary party in which every member needed to be both a theoretician and a practising revolutionary. He suggested that:

> *...all members of a political party should be regarded as intellectuals and the revolutionary party must 'work incessantly to raise the intellectual level of ever-growing strata of the populace, to give a personality to the amorphous mass element'.[4]*

The practical element of Marxism has suffered two huge blows in this century. Le Blanc quite rightly lays the blame for this on reformism and Stalinism. He argues:

This disjuncture between theory and practice flows, in large measure, from an acceptance of Marx's general analyses and a rejection of his actual revolutionary-democratic strategic orientation within the organised workers' movement for many years. Marx's actual political orientation was abandoned due to the ascendancy of the reformist bureaucratism of social democracy in various forms and also due to the ascendancy of the brutal authoritarianism of Stalinism in its various incarnations.[5]

The arguments against reformism and Stalinism posed by revolutionary socialists are a defence and vindication of the ideas of Marx and Engels. For example, Le Blanc refers to Trotsky who understood most clearly that his fight against Stalin was also one in which the revolutionary ideas of Marx and Lenin were in contest. Trotsky explained in a 1937 interview in the US press, 'In the name of a fight against "Trotskyism" the [Stalinist] bureaucracy combats and slanders the revolutionary essence of the teaching of Marx and Lenin'.[6]

Alongside reformism and Stalinism may be added a third dimension which, although not of the same weight and significance, would also undermine the central pivot of Marxist thought. This third force was academic Marxism and was in fact anticipated by Trotsky who declared, 'The essence of Marx and Engels' activity was that they theoretically anticipated and prepared the way for the age of proletarian revolution. If this is set aside, we end up with nothing but academic Marxism, that is, the most repulsive caricature'.[7] Le Blanc chooses Perry Anderson to describe academic Marxism

...a seclusion of theorists in universities far from the life of the proletariat in their own countries, and a contraction of theory from economics and politics into philosophy. This specialisation was accompanied by an increasing difficulty in language, whose technical barriers were a function of its distance from the masses... The loss of any dynamic contact working class practice in turn displaced Marxist theory towards contemporary non-Marxist and idealist systems of thought, with which it now typically developed in close if contradictory symbiosis.[8]

In chapter one of *From Marx to Gramsci* Le Blanc also mentions some of the key figures in the 20th century who have claimed to be Marxists, such as Mao in China and Castro in Cuba. There is not the space here to discuss these in any depth but it is worth showing how Le Blanc dismisses these so called variants of Marxism in all their disguises:

The question is not whether Marx's ideas generated an impressive array of influential and interesting perspectives. We can see that they did. Instead we

*must ask whether the central Marxist category of **proletarian revolution**—the working class rising up, smashing the bourgeois state, establishing its own political power, and maintaining that power in order to transform society along socialist lines—corresponds to some significant measure of historical reality. In the light of this question, many of the variants and interpretations of Marxism fade into the shadows.*[9]

In light of this it is surprising that Le Blanc then distinguishes between *Marxists* (someone operating within a Marxist theoretical framework) and *revolutionary Marxists* (someone who embraces a particular approach to politics consistent with Marx's own, quite specific, revolutionary political orientation). This appears to be a neat excuse for those Marxists who prefer to read books rather than encounter the arguments, debates and practical experiences of working class people. If the contention of Le Blanc's book is that there should be no disjuncture between theory and practice, then it seems clear that Marxists should do two things. First, books are read, re-read and written to develop a theoretical understanding of the world, and second, we fight practically to make revolutionary action a reality.

Theory of capitalist development

Marx is perhaps at his best describing the dynamics, contradictions and crises of capitalism. Chapter two of this book explores a Marxist understanding of how capitalism works.

According to Marx and Engels crises do not only occur in one country but, due to the global nature of capitalism, they create global eruptions, or as Luxemburg suggests when analysing the effects of imperialism, 'a chain of economic catastrophes: world crises, wars, revolution',[10] in all parts of the world. The current conjecture about the globalisation of capitalism is not 'a new discovery'. Over 150 years ago Marx and Engels saw only too clearly how capitalism spread to all corners of the globe. It is worth quoting in full Marx and Engels' description of how capitalism spreads:

> *Modern industry has established the world market, for which the discovery of America paved the way... The bourgeoisie has through its exploitation of the world market given a cosmopolitan character to production and consumption in every country... All old-established national industries have been destroyed or are daily being destroyed. They are dislodged by new industries, whose introduction becomes a life and death question for all civilised nations, by industries that no longer work up indigenous raw material, but raw material drawn from the remotest zones; industries whose products are consumed, not only at home, but in every quarter of the globe. In place of the old wants,*

satisfied by the productions of the country, we find new wants, requiring for their satisfaction the products of distant lands and climes... The bourgeoisie, by the rapid improvement of all instruments of production, by the immensely facilitated means of communication, draws all, even the most barbarian, nations into civilisation. The cheap prices of its commodities are the heavy artillery with which it batters down all Chinese walls, with which it forces the barbarians' intensely obstinate hatred of foreigners to capitulate. It compels all nations on pain of extinction to adopt the bourgeois mode of production; it compels them to introduce what it calls civilisation into their midst, ie, to become bourgeois themselves. In one word, it creates a world after its own image.[11]

Le Blanc points out that the spread of capitalism across the globe was not tantamount to 'progress'. He chooses a quotation from Rosa Luxemburg to depict the real cost of capitalist expansion. She explains:

To the capitalist economists and politicians, railroads, matches, sewerage systems and warehouses are progress and culture. Of themselves such works, grafted upon primitive conditions, are neither culture nor progress, for they are too dearly paid for with the sudden economic and cultural ruin of the peoples who must drink down the bitter cup of misery and horror of two social orders, of traditional agricultural landlordism, of supermodern, super-refined capitalist exploitation, at one and the same time.[12]

Karl Kautsky, however, in opposing Luxemburg and Lenin's analysis of imperialism, actually thought capitalist expansion brought society closer to socialism. He suggests 'the more a state is capitalistic on the one hand and democratic on the other, the nearer it is to socialism'.[13] Kautsky also believed that advanced capitalists would establish 'ultra-imperialism' which according to him was:

...a planetary economy controlled by a unified elite of scientifically trained managers who have left the national state behind and merged their separate identities in the formation of a global cartel linking all the industrially advanced centres of the world.[14]

This is a far cry from both Lenin and Luxemburg's conception of destruction, exploitation, oppression and devastating world wars culminating from imperialist rivalries between nations. It is also in total contradiction to how Marx and Engels predicted the future. They believed that the conflict between bosses and workers across the world would end 'either in a revolutionary reconstitution of society at large, or in the common ruin of the contending classes'.[15]

Beginning from the premise that capitalism was spreading across the globe, Marx began to assess what this meant for socialist revolution. He recognised that for socialism to be successful there needed to be enough productive capacity to provide people with the goods and services that they both needed and desired. Socialism was indeed made possible because capitalism had unleashed the necessary productive powers.

On this contention, capitalist development was a necessary precondition for the rise of socialism. Marx and Engels in fact traced the different modes of production which had evolved in the West to evidence five stages of development: primitive communism, slave society, feudalism, capitalism and socialism. But as Le Blanc points out, this 'stages' theory of development was incorrectly interpreted by Kautsky, Plekanov ('the father of Russian Marxism'), and, in the early 1900s, Lenin (who later reassessed his understanding of capitalist development) to mean that Russia would first have to go through a bourgeois revolution before it could have a socialist revolution. Le Blanc cites a letter published in a Russian journal written in 1877 by Marx to prove that Marx rejected this interpretation of his ideas. Marx did not believe that countries had to fatalistically go through these stages to get to socialism. In this letter he explicitly warned against 'transforming my historical sketch of the genesis of capitalism in Western Europe into a historico-philosophical theory of the general course fatally imposed on all peoples, whatever the historical circumstances in which they find themselves placed'.[16]

With reference to Russia, Marx showed quite bluntly how 'stages' were not necessary:

> *Did Russia have to undergo a long Western-style incubation of mechanical industry before it could make use of machinery, steamships, railways etc? Let them also explain how they managed to introduce, in the twinkling of an eye, that whole machinery of exchange (banks, credit companies, etc) which was the work of centuries in the West.*[17]

As Le Blanc reports, the first Marxist of the 20th century to offer a clearly formulated challenge to this unilinear stages view was Leon Trotsky. Trotsky agreed with the classical Marxist view that socialism could not survive in an economically underdeveloped country, but 'a national revolution is not a self-contained whole; it is only a link in the international chain. The international constitutes a permanent process, despite temporary declines and ebbs'.[18] Trotsky contended in 1905 that the:

> *Russian Revolution is a 'bourgeois' revolution because it sets out to liberate bourgeois society from the chains and fetters of absolutism and feudal ownership. But the principal driving force is the proletariat, and that is why, so*

far as its method is concerned, it is a proletarian revolution .[19]

The global nature of capitalism meant it was possible to overcome the economic backwardness of an individual country, as long as the revolution spread across national borders: socialist revolution was possible in Russia. As Le Blanc points out, by 1917 Lenin too had drawn the same conclusions.

Theory of the labour movement

If the future was either socialist revolution or ruination for humankind the question of what workers are capable of comes to the fore. Le Blanc spends two chapters examining whether workers can develop the necessary revolutionary consciousness and practice required in order to bring a socialist revolution to fruition. He begins by arguing that economic struggles may quickly turn into political struggles. For example, as Marx explained:

> *The attempt to obtain forcibly from individual capitalists a shortening of the working hours in some individual factory or some individual trade by means of a strike, etc, is a purely economic movement. On the other hand, a movement forcibly to obtain an eight hour law, etc, is a political movement...in this way a **political** movement grows everywhere out of the individual economic movement of the workers.*[20]

Although every economic struggle had the potential to lead to political confrontation, this was under no circumstances an inevitable progression. Gramsci in particular recognised that 'politics always lags behind economics, far behind'.[21] Even during huge social and economic crises, revolution is never automatic.

One major reason for the containment of revolutionary struggles was the hold exercised on workers by reformist trade union leaders and social democratic parties like the Labour Party in Britain. Lenin, Luxemburg and Trotsky each wrote about the dangers of reformism at the turn of the century when it was a relatively new phenomenon. Their insight and understanding of the reformist movement has tremendous clarity and sharpness. With reference to German reformism, Luxemburg wrote as early as 1890:

> *It was characteristic of party conditions at the time that the socialist parliamentarians should have the decisive word alike in theory and practice... frittering away the energies of the labour movement... What passed officially for Marxism became a cloak for all possible kinds of opportunism, for persistent shirking of the revolutionary class struggle, for every conceivable half*

measure. Thus the German social democracy, and the labour movement, the trade union movement as well, were condemned to pine away within the framework of capitalist society.[22]

Lenin argued in strong terms that to create political confrontation workers have to learn to respond with genuine revolutionary consciousness and understanding. He argued:

*Working class consciousness cannot be genuine political consciousness unless the workers are trained to respond to **all** cases of tyranny, oppression, violence and abuse, no matter **what class** is affected—unless they are trained, moreover, to respond from a social democratic [a revolutionary socialist] point of view and no other. The consciousness of the working masses cannot be genuine class consciousness unless the workers learn, from concrete and above all from topical political facts and events, to observe **every** other social class in **all** the manifestations of its intellectual, ethical and political life; unless they learn to apply in practice the materialist analysis and the materialist estimate of **all** aspects of the life and activity of **all** classes, strata, and groups of the population. Those who concentrate the attention, observation, and consciousness of the working class exclusively, or even mainly, upon itself alone are not social democrats; for the self knowledge of the working class is indissolubly bound up, not solely with the clear theoretical understanding—or rather, not so much with the theoretical, as with the practical understanding—of the relationships between **all** the various classes of modern society, acquired through the experience of political life.*[23]

This political training could not come from trade unions or reformist organisations but could only be established through a revolutionary party. For example, with reference to trade unions, Trotsky expressed, 'Trade unions do not offer, and in line with their task, composition and manner of recruiting membership, cannot offer a finished revolutionary programme; in consequence, they cannot replace the party'.[24]

Unfortunately, Le Blanc does not give sufficient emphasis to the role of the revolutionary party. This is perhaps one of the book's main weaknesses, since both Lenin and Trotsky in particular, paid close attention to the role of the party.

Does revolutionary Marxism have a future?

One of the book's most interesting and thought provoking chapters is Le Blanc's consideration of whether revolutionary Marxism has a future. To what extent, he asks, is a workers' state as envisioned by the revolutionary Marxists a genuine possibility? Le Blanc does not attempt to skirt round the difficulties which revolutionaries have faced in their attempts to make socialist revolution a reality. He begins with a brief discussion of the immense difficulties encountered by the Bolshevik Party in Russia in the 1920s. The rise of Stalin and the consequent destruction of any chance for socialism to develop on a world scale is perhaps the greatest defeat revolutionary socialists have ever suffered. Le Blanc, however, quite correctly argues that there was nothing inevitable about the rise of Stalin and that one of the main lessons to be learnt from history is that socialism can only be realised on a world scale and not, as Stalin argued, in one country.

Alongside the hundreds and thousands of revolutionaries and activists murdered by Stalin, were those who were being slaughtered by Nazi violence. Writing in 1936, Trotsky observed that, 'Not a revolutionary grouping in world history has yet experienced such terrible pressure'.[25] He predicted a second world war where destruction, hunger, epidemics and savagery were on a far greater scale than ever before, but he also added that revolutionary parties 'may also be formed considerably later, in a number of years, in the midst of the ruins and the accumulation of debris following upon the victory of fascism and war'.[26]

After the Second World War, the advanced Western capitalist countries experienced an economic boom. This meant that when workers demanded an improvement in their standard of living (even in an economic boom workers often had to take strike action to win a pay rise), the system as a whole could afford to meet their demands without cutting too much into the profits of the ruling class. In these circumstances the success of reform had a conservatising effect on workers' consciousness. This period, however, as Le Blanc acknowledges, has without question, come to an end. A consequence of an end to economic prosperity is that the road to reform is closing.

Unfortunately, Le Blanc's final comment on whether revolutionary Marxism has a future is that 'its project is in a shambles'.[27]He contends, 'that there is an "unevenness" in the consciousness—and in the circumstances—of the various sectors of the working class which facilitates the fragmentation of the working class and the defeat of each of the fragments'.[28]

We are left with Le Blanc's assessment of the contribution that Marxism has made: it is 'one of the most comprehensive and intellectually powerful prescriptions for social change ever developed, the perspective elaborated in various ways by Marx and Engels, Luxemburg, Lenin, Trotsky, and Gramsci adds up to an approach to reality and a body of thought which is irreplaceable for those wishing to come to grips with the past and the future'.[29]Yet Le Blanc closes his analysis by concluding that revolution is extremely unlikely. Those of us who are more optimistic about the prospects for revolution will read these works as they were intended, as a *guide to action*.

Notes
1   P Le Blanc (ed), *From Marx to Gramsci* (Humanities Press, 1996), p8.
2   Ibid, px.
3   Ibid, pp2-3.
4   Ibid, p58.
5   Ibid, pix.
6   Ibid, px.
7   Ibid, p45.
8   Ibid, p13.
9   Ibid, p17.
10   Ibid, p33.
11   Ibid, p27.
12   Ibid, p32.
13   Ibid, p36.
14   Ibid, p36.
15   Ibid, p45.
16   Ibid, p29.
17   Ibid, p31.
18   Ibid, pp38-40.
19   Ibid, pp38-39.
20   Ibid, pp47-48.
21   Ibid, p23.
22   Ibid, p53.
23   Ibid, pp48-49.
24   Ibid, p50.
25   Ibid, p107.
26   Ibid, p107.
27   Ibid, p35.
28   Ibid, p119.
29   Ibid, pp118-119.

Review article: Labour's history of hope and betrayal

A review of Keith Laybourn, **The Rise of Socialism in Britain** *(Sutton Publishing, 1997), Daniel Weinbren,* **Generating Socialism: Recollections of Life in the Labour Party** *(Sutton Publishing, 1997), Steven Fielding,* **The Labour Party: 'Socialism' and Society since 1951** *(Manchester University Press, 1997).*

CHRIS BAMBERY

In the 1960s I remember that once every month someone used to call round to collect my father's Labour Party dues. The Edinburgh East constituency was one of only two in the city held by Labour. Today Labour hold every parliamentary seat in Edinburgh, but I wonder if they have the same grass roots organisation as they did in the 1960s. Three new books about the history of Labour give some insight into how Labour won the support of workers, and how that faith in Labour can be challenged in the future.

Keith Laybourn's *The Rise of Socialism in Britain* is an examination of left wing politics in Britain between 1891 and 1951. This volume aims to give a summary of various views on the development of socialist politics. But it eventually reinforces the notion that Marxism has never found a home inside the British working class.

The first Marxist organisation in Britain was the Social Democratic Federation. The SDF formally accepted Marxism in 1884 yet it drew bitter criticism from both Marx and Engels. Its autocratic leader, H M Hyndman, championed a mechanical Marxism combined with a strong dose of British nationalism. Engels was enraged when the SDF's sectarianism left it incapable of seizing the opportunities open to it in the upsurge of New Unionism in the 1880s.

Indeed the SDF's membership fell from 6,744 members organised in 40 branches in 1889, to 453 members grouped in 34 branches a year later, and this at the height of the New Unionism.[1] In 1889 SDF members were instructed to tell workers that strike pay would be better spent on socialist propaganda and that strikes were a diversion from the quest for socialism. The SDF's nine point programme issued in 1889 made no reference to trade unions or the strikes taking place. Little wonder Engels wrote that they were 'a mere sect because they cannot conceive that living theory of action, of working with the working classes at every possible stage of its development'.[2] Yet for all its immense faults the SDF did, against the odds, introduce a generation of working class activists to Marxist ideas. When working class struggle rose again, in the Great Unrest of 1910-1914, many of the key activists had been members of the SDF or had contact with it.   *Social Democ Fed*

However, the failure of the SDF to orientate on the militancy of the New Unionism contributed to a political vacuum among newly radicalised workers. As the balance of forces shifted and management moved onto the offensive workers were forced to look for a political alternative. In Bradford in 1891 the management of Manningham Mills imposed a 25 percent wage cut on their workforce. The town polarised between the employers and middle classes on the one hand and the town's working class, and indeed the working class of Yorkshire and the north, on the other. The Liberals, who ran the Watch Committee and until then had enjoyed trade union support, prevented strikers holding meetings in the town centre and, as clashes developed, drafted in police and soldiers with the Riot Act being read on 13 April. A month afterwards, in the wake of a bitter defeat, the strike leaders presided over a meeting to form the Independent Labour Party in opposition to the Liberals. The next two years saw the creation of similar parties across Yorkshire and Lancashire.

The ILP emerged as a national organisation with a membership of between 35,000 and 50,000 by 1895. In that year the Bradford ILP had 2,000 members grouped across the town in 29 ILP groups or clubs. By 1898 it had a fee paying membership of between 11,000 and 13,000.[3] The sales of Robert Blatchford's *The Clarion*, which reached 80,000, give some sense of the potential audience for socialism. The paper and the associated Clarion Scouts organisation focused on the creation of a different working class social and cultural world with cycle clubs and so on.

The ILP leadership manoeuvred against unity with other socialists. Instead, Keir Hardie and those around him had a clear vision of the direction in which the ILP had to develop—by creating a new Labour alliance with the trade unions. The trade union leaders had until then been champions of working class support for the Liberals. By the 1890s their allegiance to what had been the dominant party of British capitalism was under strain. Under a Tory government there was a growing sense that British manufacturing was losing ground to its German and American rivals and that their solution was to launch an employers' offensive. This involved placing legal shackles on the unions. In 1896 picketing was effectively made illegal once more (a view upheld in the high court three years later). The strongest union, the craft Amalgamated Society of Engineers, was defeated in the 1897-1898 lockout.

Trade union officialdom increasingly began to see that they could not rely on Liberal politicians and that they needed their own representatives in Westminster. Politically this shift towards independent working class representation did not imply a break with the assumptions underlying the old support for the Liberals. In 1889 the TUC accepted a motion to increase the number of Labour MPs in parliament but only by a narrow majority. In February 1900 the TUC hosted a meeting between those unions which supported this motion and the ILP, the SDF and the Fabians to launch the Labour Representation Committee—the fore-runner of today's Labour Party.

The LRC's growth was spurred by the Taff Vale judgement 1901. The rail union was made liable for a South Wales rail company's losses during a strike. Every union's funds were now open to such an attack. In response trade union officials looked to secure their own representatives within the parliamentary system. Trade union affiliation to the LRC grew from 350,000 in early 1901 to 861,000 by 1903.

Laybourn's book charts the development of the Labour Party through its initial breakthrough in the 1906 election when a pact with the winning Liberals gave it 30 seats. On his way he significantly downplays the Great Unrest and the shop stewards organisation which developed in the war years. The Communist Party's failure to emerge as a serious opposition to the Labour Party during the 1930s is used as further evidence of the failure of Marxism to win popular support in Britain. Yet during the years between 1936 and 1939 the Communist Party's popular front line meant it was in many essentials formally to the right of the Labour Party. Keith Laybourn raises criticisms of Labour's record which many socialists could agree with, but the criticisms are accompanied by the idea that there was no possible alternative to Labourism.

When its membership was at its peak the Labour Party still had networks of local members who counted for something in their communities and workplaces. *Generating Socialism* gives you a real sense of that. It also shows you how Labour built its support at grassroots level in the first half of this century.

Much of Labour's growth centred on activity. In the 1930s, for example, Labour activists interviewed in the book organised successful rent strikes among private tenants in Kingston and Norbiton.[4] A picture of how activists built Ealing North constituency in a new industrial suburb provides a fresh alternative to the Peter Mandelson approach to politics:

We used to have early morning factory-gate meetings at Hoover's. I remember going to Hoover's with Bill Molley at about quarter-past six in the morning so that we would meet the night-shift coming off work. There were large factories; we used to have factory-gate meetings at Lyons and in the Greenford area, on Perivale estate, lunch-time meetings... We had a large number of trade union reps on the GMC, and they were also quite generous to the party... The party was very sort of buoyant... Ealing North was a thriving constituency... The party used to have mass canvasses in those days and Sunday mornings was devoted to a given area. Probably 20 people would converge on an area and canvass, which doesn't happen now. We used to have a lot of public meetings, a large number of public meetings at that time and always got good attendances.[5]

In Newham one member recalls, 'You could get hold of [Councillor] Tommy [Groves] at any time of the day or night. If he was out in the street he'd talk to you. If you went to his house, no matter what he was doing, he'd take you in.' In Ilford one woman remembers that councillors 'were always walking around'.[6] Today many Labour councillors have no roots in the area they represent and would never be seen on the streets of their ward.

There was also a vibrant Labour press. The Co-operative's paper, *Reynolds News*, had sales of over 400,000 in 1937 and climbed to a peak of 712,000 in 1951.[7] The local Labour Party branches were also often well organised. In the unlikely setting of Chichester, Sussex, the Labour Party had three full time constituency officers in 1955: an agent, a secretary and a fundraiser who organised a tote.[8] In 1959 the Faversham and Lanark Labour parties both had individual memberships of over 4000.[9] One member, looking back to the election of the Attlee government, reminisces:

The question of recruiting members in 1945 is easy, we made hundreds of them. Now, ideally, if you take a ward and it consists of say 50 roads, you can split that up into areas and, if you're luckier still, you take every road of those 50 and you can have a street captain. Now, that street captain knows the road and knows the people. So when you come to polling day he [sic] goes along and knocks on the doors and says 'You know you're Labour and it's voting and you'll be along there, won't you?' and that, of course, is the ideal basis of Labour Party organisation which, regretfully, I don't ever see coming back again.[10]

These local networks ensured that Labour membership was carried on down through the generations. A 1958 survey of party members in Manchester showed 58 percent had a relative who was interested in politics and 77 percent were union members.[11]

Generating Socialism gives a wonderful view of working class life between the wars, one sometimes at variance with the traditional view of Britain as an island of stability. One woman recalls going as a teenager to a Labour Party rally in Ilford which was broken up by the fascists:

> And my mind goes back to it now that I saw grey-haired women up there shaking the Union Jack, you know, and 'We want Hitler! We want Hitler!' and the fascist salute. And you know it frightened me. Not for the violence, but for people's thoughts... That's when I changed my mind about Great Britain. You're not what I thought you were. Because there were these people who were willing to co-operate with Hitler.[12]

Yet there is an important contemporary thread running through *Generating Socialism*. It both serves as a riposte to Blair and Mandelson, and offers hope to those who might despair of their allegiance to Labour. Tony Benn, in his introduction, argues:

> But the overwhelming impression given in these recollections is of goodwill and comradeship that has characterised our co-operation together from the very beginning and of the immense amount of work that was—and still is— undertaken by local parties... Those who read the memories contained in this book will find it impossible to believe that the Labour and trade union movement and its rank and file members are ready to fade away to make room for the pollsters and the advertising agents whose only constituents seem to be the media proprietors, editors and correspondents.[13]

For those who have heard Tony Benn respond to questions about Blair's hold on the Labour Party this has a familiar ring. Underneath, he argues, the Labour Party remains fundamentally sound—Blair's hold is episodic and the fundamental nature of the Labour Party will win out in the end. The bottom line, of course, is that you've got to stick in the Labour Party though thick and thin.

That argument rests on a simple truth. The rank and file of the Labour Party does contain some of the finest people you could meet—like the people interviewed here who fought fascism in the 1930s, supported the Spanish Republic against Franco, opposed racism, kept the torch alight in the fight against apartheid and so on. *Generating Socialism* is an inspiring read precisely because it expresses their experiences. Yet it is necessary to go beyond the warm glow of solidarity emanating from this volume.

For socialists critical of the Labourist tradition it is interesting that the only strikes mentioned are the 1926 General Strike and, more fleetingly, the 1984-1985 Miners' Strike. Both were so seismic that they created a huge response among Labour's grass roots (although in 1984 that was delayed until the European elections were out of the way). The chapter on the 1926 General Strike is excellent. One future Communist Party member remembered middle class strikebreakers being chased down Hackney's Mare Street and dumped in a horse trough. Syd Bidwell recalls, 'My father was on the General Strike local committee. I was very young, but I recall the workers attacking buses at the Southall bus garage...and pushing a bus over—the crowd pushing the bus right over on its side, and it was being driven by a blackleg student'.[14] Another Kingston Labour Party member recalled:

> *My early political contacts occurred first of all in 1926, during the General Strike, when my eldest brother took me to Hyde Park, where the demonstrations were occurring. I have vivid memories of the rough treatment of the strikers by the police, with arms painfully twisted up behind their backs. Even at the age of 11, I could begin to see the class struggle.*[15]

But what this book ignores is that the leadership of the Labour Party loathed both strikes. Similarly they opposed the mobilisations against Mosley and the unemployed marches. A Ministry of Health report noted that in Plymouth the Salvation Army had to feed that section of the 1932 march because 'the Labour Party gave no support to the marchers, who were unable to collect a halfpenny'.[16]

The Labour Party was intimately connected to the working class through the unions. But it was always at a remove from the class struggle. Underlying that is a separation between economics and politics which itself reflects how capitalist democracy functions. We have democratic control over very limited sectors of the state, but no control or even say over the workings of the market. The Labour Party is about operating solely within the confines of that narrow political democracy while the trade unions are about defending workers' economic position. The idea that workers might use their economic muscle to bring about political change is dismissed out of hand. This separation between economics and politics can lead to crazy situations where Labour activists find themselves wearing different hats in different situations, as a Chester Labour Party member recalls:

> *We had a particular item of business and a very well known and quite well revered man in the Chester labour movement, a chap called Alderman Ted Ashton, got up. I said 'Alderman Ashton, you can't speak on this business.' 'What?' he said. 'I can't speak on this business? It's got to deal with the railways,' he said. I said, 'Yes, I know.' He said, 'I'm the branch secretary of the NUR. What do you mean I can't speak on it?' I said, 'Because you are here as*

*the delegate from Broughton Ward Labour Party, you are not a delegate from
the NUR here.' 'Oh, bloody ridiculous.' He came to me later and said, 'You
were quite right.'* [17]

Even in the area of challenging fascism and racism, the lack of an
ideological clarity comes through. In 1964 the sitting Labour MP for
Southall called for 'a complete ban on immigration to Southall' which
opened the door to the British National Party (later relaunched as the
National Front) which stood against him on a platform of a complete ban
on 'coloured immigration' and on benefits for immigrants. The Nazis
won 9 percent of the vote. Jimmy Allison, who rose to become Scottish
organiser of the Labour Party, recalls the racist views of Bermondsey
MP Bob Mellish, who also championed the Spanish fascist dictator
Franco.[18]

Similarly there was great diversity on the question of women's role in
the party. From 1918 onwards women were organised into separate
Women's Sections which had no formal power. In the 1920s Winnie
Smith started one such Women's Section. She recalls:

*Men were the masters and women were left to do the soppy things... Then I
found out the Women's Sections were just expected to do the drying up, the
washing up, run the raffles, but they were never involved in politics at all, and
they were never given the freedom to do so. They could never come out can-
vassing and they were not allowed to speak. Men looked down on them as
idiots or just women for the kitchen only.*

The Labour Party also encourages a slavish devotion to parliament
which even infects those on the left of the party. Aneurin Bevan writing
in praise of the British parliament in *In Place of Fear* in 1952, argued the
following:

*The absence of a written constitution gives British politics a flexibility
enjoyed by few nations. No courts can construe the power of the British parliament. It interprets its own authority, and from it there is no appeal. This
gives it a revolutionary quality, and enables us to entertain the hope of
bringing about social transformations, without the agony and prolonged
crises experienced by other nations.* [19]

Generating Socialism effectively ends with the finale of the 1945
election, the continuing support of veteran members for the party, and
their pride in the welfare state. Despite its strengths, this book offers no
explanation as to what happened next, and why Labour membership was
to fall so dramatically.

In 1952 individual membership of the Labour Party—as opposed to the number of trade unionists who were affiliated to ¿—stood at just over 1 million. By the early 1980s that figure dropped to around the 250,000 mark. Today it claims 350,000.[20] The only national survey of its membership found that in 1992 Labour's membership was 96 percent white, 61 percent male, that 65 percent were white collar and professional workers, with 62 percent of members employed in the public sector and 52 percent over the age of 45.[21] To explain this, we have to turn to Labour's record in the 1960s and 1970s and Fielding's book, *The Labour Party: Socialism and society since 1951*, provides a few pointers. Fielding brings together an interesting set of documents and memoirs covering the party's evolution from its post-war victory up to 1995.

In the 1960s a radicalisation began among Labour's Young Socialists, receiving an impetus from the movement against nuclear weapons. A 1965 survey of Young Socialists found that there was a continuity with earlier periods of radicalisation:

> *The further left a Young Socialist, the more likely he [sic] is to have actively radical, if not revolutionary parents, parents whose own politics were shaped in 1917, 1926 or 1931...of those who are active the great majority are merely continuing a family habit of enjoyment in public affairs. Often the critical politicising experiences that brought the family into politics lie three generations away, the Docks Strike [1889], the Revolution of 1905, the Great War.[22]*

However, when that radicalisation spread under the1964-1970 Labour government led by Harold Wilson it was channelled into directions independent of the Labour Party. So 1968 is seen as the year of student protests—but it also marked the rebirth of revolutionary politics. By 1969 and 1970 there was also a mushrooming of industrial militancy which meant many groups of workers looked to their own economic power and shop stewards organisations.

The 1974-1979 Labour government spawned even greater disillusionment but industrial confidence was undermined by the recession and the effects of Labour's Social Contract. When it came to the 1984-1985 Miners' Strike the Labour left was still strong enough to experience a revival. While the Labour leadership stood aloof from the strike, constituency banners were there on the marches for the miners, and local Labour activists were important to building local support groups. One member in Woking reveals, 'The party came to life: we had something practical to work on, we had a cause.' Brighton Labour Party reported that 'many inactive members got involved in our collections and started coming to meetings again, and new members joined'.[23]

But with the end of the strike the Labour Party began to retreat further from struggle and effective campaigning. By the 1990s the great campaigns against the poll tax, the Gulf War, the Nazis and the Criminal Justice Bill mobilised many thousands of Labour supporters but with less and less evidence of an organised Labour presence. On the contrary, revolutionaries built those campaigns in the face of hostility from the Labour leadership.

This wasn't something entirely new. In the 1930s the Communist Party did something similar when it opposed Mosley's fascists, organised aid for Spain and built union organisation in the 'new industries'. The Communist Party is repeatedly mentioned in *Generating Socialism* but only in soft focus. The former Communists interviewed here remind us that the CP recruited the cream of the British working class in the 1930s. But the 1945 cut-off point means the Stalinist nature of that party and its slavish support of Stalin are obscured. Stalinism provided the Labour left with a degree of ideological cement. The Communist Party could provide a top down model of how 'socialism' could be achieved using the state. Indeed by the 1960s the Communist Party almost gloried in its portrayal of itself as providing the industrial muscle for the parliamentarians of the Labour left.

Today's Labour leaders would no doubt discount *Generating Socialism* as nostalgia. Many Blairites do have a pro-Communist past (I think in particular of one defence minister speaking passionately in defence of Cuban intervention in Angola at a Scottish NUS conference). But for all of them, as with Blair's attitude to his past membership of CND, that was then and this is now. Everyone interviewed in the book, from Tony Benn to Tony Blair, agrees on one thing: there is no alternative to the Labour Party.

To pick up the threads left by *Generating Socialism*, we have to return to Steven Fielding's *The Labour Party: 'Socialism' and Society since 1951*. Looking back on the Attlee government in 1952 Richard Crossman noted, 'Yet, after scarcely four years in office, the government had fulfilled its historic mission. The nationalisation of half a dozen major industries, the construction of an all-in system of social security and a free health service, and a tentative application of planning to the national economy—the achievement of these reforms seemed to have exhausted the content of British socialism.'

There were two responses to the defeat of the Attlee government in 1951. One was to support a policy of continuing nationalisation which crystallised round left wing rebel Aneurin Bevan. The other was to call for a profound revision of Labour's policies, and in particular the dropping of any further nationalisation. This position was championed by the new Labour leader, Hugh Gaitskell. The right was supported by the block votes of the biggest unions at Labour's conference. Right wingers, like the future founder of the Social Democratic Party, Bill Rogers, rejected calls for greater democracy in the party and defended the block vote he would later so bitterly denounce.[24]

By 1956 Anthony Crosland was arguing in *The Future of Socialism* that 'capitalism had been transformed out of recognition'. He predicted the post-war boom would continue until any economic reasons for socialism had been eradicated. Crosland quoted former Labour premier Lord Attlee who said 'I joined the socialist movement because I did not like the kind of society we had and I wanted something better' but Crosland then asked, 'Why should anyone say the same today?'[25] The right wing *Socialist Commentary* explained that 'both parties [Labour and the Tories] have gradually been pushed further towards the centre. The battle for the floating vote—which fluctuates somewhere in the centre, or in the case of non-voters is stationary there—remains as the only method of changing the parliamentary position, unsatisfactory as it is for both parties'.[26]

The left round Bevan and *Tribune* continued to argue that Labour could win with a bolder policy. Bevan made his peace with Gaitskell in 1956 and the following year, as shadow foreign minister, spoke out against nuclear disarmament at party conference. The internal fights became more acrimonious culminating in two great pitched battles— over Gaitskell's attempt to drop Clause Four of the party's constitution and then over nuclear disarmament at the 1960 and 1961 annual confer- ences. Gaitskell was defeated over Clause Four but, after losing at the 1960 conference, won over nuclear disarmament the following year.

In January 1963 Gaitskell suddenly died. The next month Harold Wilson, seen as the left candidate, beat the right winger George Brown to become party leader. Crossman records how Wilson was a guest at a dinner given by Barbara Castle and attended by the main figures on the left of the party. He told them, 'You must understand that I am running a Bolshevik Revolution with a Tsarist shadow cabinet'.[27]

Wilson scraped into office in 1964 campaigning for a 'New Britain' which would end 13 'wasted years' of Tory rule. In March 1966 he called an election which gave him a 96 seat majority. For the previous two years Wilson and his chancellor, James Callaghan, had refused to devalue ster- ling which was overpriced on the world money markets. Immediately after the election there was a bitter seafarers' strike. The bosses were pre- pared to settle, but Wilson encouraged them to dig their heels in, and used a red smear against the strike leaders. The strike gave rise to a run on ster- ling. In July 1966 Wilson, still refusing to devalue, was forced to cut public spending, increase taxes and limit wages in order to reassure the markets. Wilson only secured a narrow majority in the cabinet and there was fierce battle at Labour's national executive between Wilson and Callaghan on the one side and the union leaders on the other.

This episode marked the end of Labour's honeymoon and heralded a rapid change of fortunes. Steven Fielding has done particularly well in selecting material which shows the process of disillusionment among Labour members. In Newton Heath, Manchester, attendances at the ward Labour Party declined from an average attendance of 30 in 1965 to 25 in the following year, 18 in 1967, and 9 in 1968 before reviving to 16 in 1969 and then slumping back to 11 in 1970 (an election year).[28] In the Northfield constituency, 'Mr Elkington commented on the general feeling of apathy within the ward. Small attendances were being recorded at meetings, even though speakers had been arranged'.[29]

One response to Labour's unpopularity was to look for scapegoats as working class living standards fell. The minutes for Bedford Divisional Labour Party's October 1967 meeting show how this affected Labour members:

> *A member said that we might just as well 'give the whole damn country to the blacks, as they would get it in the end anyway. Before long we would have a black king on the throne and then it would be God help us! The poor old white man might just as well emigrate and leave the place to them'... Mr Storrow said he was not aware that Ian Smith* [the white supremacist head of Rhodesia] *was present but apparently he was...*

In February 1968 the Labour government introduced the Commonwealth Immigrants Bill, an emergency measure, blocking entry to the country by Kenyan Asians holding British passports. This followed a vicious campaign whipped up by the right wing press and the Tories, in the face of which Wilson collapsed. But opposition was beginning to form on the left, independent of the Labour Party, firstly to the Vietnam War and then to a wages freeze.

This had an effect within Labour's grass roots as the following letter to a local paper by a longstanding member of the Stalybridge and Hyde Labour Party, written in July 1968, shows:

> *I have been a full time agent for the Labour Party and I have conducted two parliamentary elections in my present constituency. But I can no longer work for the return of this Labour government. I have sent in my Labour Party membership card (paid up, as it was) with my resignation. What is more, I shall work within my trade union (NUPE) to secure its disaffiliation from the Labour Party. When only 23 Labour MPs can be found to oppose the penal clauses of the prices and wages legislation, what hope have we for socialism from the Parliamentary Labour Party, let alone this government? To turn the clock of history back nearly 100 years—why, I should have been surprised to find 23 Labour MPs supporting such a measure.*[30]

The Labour government fell in 1970 but was returned on a big wave of working class struggle in February 1974. The party's manifesto shows how it had to move leftwards in reaction to working class insurgency. It promised to:

a) Bring about a fundamental and irreversible shift in the balance of power and wealth in favour of working people and their families.
b) Eliminate poverty.
c) Make power in industry genuinely accountable to the workers and the community at large.
d) Achieve far greater economic equality—in income, wealth and living standards.
e) Increase social equality by giving far greater importance to full employment, housing, education and social benefits.
f) Improve the environment in which our people live and work and spend their leisure.

In return for such pledges the trade union leaders agreed to co-operate with the new Labour government in the Social Contract. Increasingly this centred on wage restraint and increasing productivity. Workers were called on to make sacrifices to restore British industry's competitiveness and unemployment mounted throughout 1975 and 1976.

Yet despite the pressures from below the trade union leaders defended the Social Contract. Jack Jones of the TGWU was key to its maintenance. In April 1975 he told the Scottish TUC:

My appeal is to respect the Social Contract, and to support it. To do this would mean advancing the interests of our members and keeping a Labour government in power. Can we really afford to let this government be thrown out? The Labour government, for all its limitations, is two hundred times better than a Tory government... How else but with unity between the trade unions and the Labour government are we going to fight rising unemployment and the redundancies that are taking place?

The Communist Party was tied to Jones and his counterpart in the engineering union, Hugh Scanlon. They were in a strong enough position to broadly contain discontent with the government by making general statements, while at a local level the Communist convenor at Leyland (now Rover) Longbridge, Derek Robinson, ordered workers to cross craft workers' picket lines, and Jimmy Airlie, the Communist convenor at Glasgow's Govan shipyard, was prepared to compete with a Polish shipyard by accepting conditions Newcastle ship workers refused to tolerate.

Fielding quotes the annual report of Warrington District Trades Council for 1977 which supported the Communist/Labour left 'alternative economic strategy'—which amounted to little more than a reheated version of the old Keynsian consensus—and had sent delegates to both the Communist initiated Liaison Committee for the Defence of Trade Unions conference in February and the National Conference for a Return to Free Collective Bargaining organised by the Leyland Combined Shop Stewards Committee in April. The former conference opposed the Social Contract but took no position on the toolroom strike at Leyland which was being attacked by their union leader, Hugh Scanlon, who backed the company locking the strikers out.

The Leyland conference was attended by 1,700 delegates including 300 Leyland stewards. A keynote speaker was the Longbridge convenor, Derek Robinson, even though he had argued for a wage rise in line with the limits set by phase two of the Social Contract. It called for an end to the Social Contract and a day of action on 20 April. But the platform attacked the toolroom strike as 'divisive' and 'sectional'. The convenor at Triumph in Coventry described the strikers as a 'sectional interest, backed by Tory newspapers, a reactionary strike'.[31] A week after the conference engineering workers at Heathrow came out over pay and were sacked. Officials of the TGWU, ASTMS and the EETPU signed a document calling on other workers to take their jobs.

The day of action on 20 April saw just 35,000 workers come out. Longbridge did not join the strike. Peter Bain from the Chrysler Linwood plant on Clydeside (the Communist Party's strongest industrial area) reported:

> I can never remember such cynicism and treachery in Communist Party politics. Their attitude is that if the trade union conferences support wage control there is nothing the rank and file can do about it...
>
> We got a 24 hour stoppage in Chrysler on 20 April. But in most of the other factories on Clydeside it was not fought for properly. The convenors of the shipyard actually called a separate stoppage against redundancies on the 19th, not the 20th.[32]

The year 1977 was a turning point not just for the Labour government but for the whole pattern of class struggle. Anger against the Social Contract had broken first with a spontaneous demonstration at Longbridge against wage controls, which led the stewards committee to call the April conference. The spring saw strikes by Leyland toolroom workers, Heathrow engineers and electricians at British Steel's Port Talbot plant. These skilled workers were all suffering from pay controls. The Labour government and the union leaders tried to portray the dis-

putes as being about well paid workers protecting their differentials at
the expense of low paid workers. The influential Communist Party
echoed this. The union officials, given crucial help from the Communist
Party among shop stewards, succeeded in isolating and dousing out the
rank and file rebellion against wage controls.

Looking back, Michael Foot, a key figure in the Labour government,
said in 1982, 'It must also be admitted that by 1977, while there was still
a large measure of support for the policy, there was also substantial
opposition especially within the labour movement'.[33] That summer saw
another decisive defeat—despite a massive mobilisation by the rank and
file. The boss of the Grunwick photo processing plant in north west
London sacked 90 Asian women after they joined a union. He was
backed by the right wing bosses' organisation, the Freedom Association.
The Grunwick strike quickly attracted massive support. The numbers
joining the picket line swelled, reaching a climax on 11 July 1977.

On that morning thousands of Yorkshire miners and dockers from
Hull, London, Merseyside and Southampton joined a mass picket
outside the plant. Cricklewood postal workers who were refusing to
handle deliveries to Grunwick walked out to join 1,000 other postal
workers on the picket line. Despite the riot police, sheer weight of
numbers prevented the scab bus getting through. The atmosphere was
like that outside Pentonville Prison and Saltley Gates in 1972.

But after the plant had been blockaded for four hours the TUC and the
strikers' union, APEX, urged people to leave the plant to join a march
round the streets of north west London. A speech by the TUC deputy
general secretary failed to move the determined pickets. Only after
Arthur Scargill of the Yorkshire NUM asked them to leave in the interests of unity did they join the march. As workers marched off to a rally in
the park the scab buses got through.

A decisive opportunity had been allowed to pass. Despite promises
from the TUC of a consumers' boycott and an effort to fight the sackings
through the court, the strike was allowed to go down to defeat. The
Labour home secretary, Merlyn Rees, continually denounced picket line
violence and publicly backed the riot police as they gained confidence to
go onto the attack. The year ended with a national strike by firefighters
over pay. The Labour government was determined to hold the line and
the TUC was determined to isolate the strike. Despite fantastic support
the strikers fought alone and the dispute eventually ended in a compromise (though at the time this appeared to be a defeat).

The Social Contact survived 1977, but pressure from below could not
be contained. Anger over pay erupted amongst the lowest paid in the
Winter of Discontent of 1978-1979. Yet these strikes were bitter and sectional in the absence of any effective leadership from either the trade

union leaders or from the shop stewards movement. That movement which had brought the Tories to their knees in 1972 and then driven them from office in 1974 effectively no longer existed.

Because it is a history of the Labour Party, Fielding's book only touches on these bitter years. Yet there is enough here to give a taste of the mood. It also demonstrates why a generation of activists, faced with the disaster of Labour in office and the erosion of shop floor confidence turned their energies towards shifting the Labour Party leftwards. Fielding's collection charts both their failure to do that and the whole process through which the right wing took control of the party, culminating in Tony Blair's launch of New Labour.

Blair's landslide victory of 1997 had a similarity with that of 1945 in that people were rejecting the past. In 1945 they were turning their backs on the 1930s and mass unemployment, poverty and the appeasement of fascism. In 1997 there was a massive rejection of the Tories' market values. But 1945 brought real reforms. In 1997 no such changes are on offer. The very size of Labour's victory has strengthened expectations and the mood for change which has existed in Britain since October 1992. Blair's New Labour is in a far weaker position than even its 1974 predecessor in that it has less roots inside the working class and it can call on no one of the stature of Jack Jones or Hugh Scanlon to carry its message into the working class. Above all, the Communist Party, which in 1977 absorbed and diffused discontent with Labour, is now dead.

The hold of Labourist politics inside the British working class was cemented by the achievements of 1945. Yet Blair's relentless drive to modernise the Labour Party, to take it towards the centre and to weaken its links with the unions, has thrown that allegiance into flux. Can British workers be drawn to a Marxist alternative? The commonsense answer to that question is no. *International Socialism* would answer that there is everything to play for.

Notes

1   K Laybourn, *The Rise of Socialism In Britain* (Sutton Publishing, 1997), p1.
2   F Engels to L Lafargue, 4 May 1991.
3   K Laybourn, op cit, p32.
4   D Weinbren, *Generating Socialism* (Sutton Publishing, 1997), p3.
5   Ibid, p169.
6   Ibid, p178.
7   Ibid, p57.
8   Ibid, p67.
9   Ibid, p185.
10   Ibid, p68.
11   Ibid, p29.
12   Ibid, p114.
13   Ibid, ppiv-v.
14   Ibid, p81.

15   Ibid, p81.
16   Ibid, p93.
17   Ibid, pp47-48.
18   Ibid, pp124-126.
19   Quoted in S Fielding (ed), *The Labour Party: 'Socialism' and Society Since 1951*
      (Manchester University Press), p34.
20   S Fielding (ed), op cit, p11.
21   P Seyd and P Whiteley, *Labour's Grass Roots* (Clarendon Press, 1992), pp28-40.
22   D Weinbren, op cit, p20.
23   Ibid, p153.
24   S Fielding, op cit, p46.
25   Ibid, pp41-43.
26   Ibid, p32.
27   Ibid, p59.
28   Ibid, pp80-81.
29   Ibid, pp82.
30   Ibid, pp85.
31   *Socialist Worker*, 9 April 1977.
32   *Socialist Worker*, 30 April 1977.
33   S Fielding, op cit, p105.

The Socialist Workers Party is one of an international grouping of socialist organisations:

AUSTRALIA: International Socialists, PO Box A338,
Sydney South

BRITAIN: Socialist Workers Party, PO Box 82, London E3

CANADA: International Socialists, PO Box 339, Station E, Toronto,
Ontario M6H 4E3

CYPRUS: Ergatiki Demokratia, PO Box 7280, Nicosia

DENMARK: Internationale Socialister, Postboks 642, 2200
København N

GREECE: Sosialistiko Ergatiko Komma, c/o Workers Solidarity, PO
Box 8161, Athens 100 10

HOLLAND: International Socialists, PO Box 9720, 3506 GR Utrecht

IRELAND: Socialist Workers Movement, PO Box 1648, Dublin 8

NEW ZEALAND:
Socialist Workers Organization, PO Box 8851, Aukland

NORWAY: Internasjonale Socialisterr, Postboks 5370, Majorstua,
0304 Oslo 3

POLAND: Solidarność Socjalistyczna, PO Box 12,
01-900 Warszawa 118

SOUTH AFRICA:
International Socialists of South Africa, PO Box 18530,
Hillbrow 2038, Johannesberg

SPAIN: Socialismo Internacional, Apartado 563, 08080, Barcelona

UNITED STATES:
International Socialist Organisation, PO Box 16085,
Chicago, Illinois 60616

ZIMBABWE:
International Socialist Organisation, PO Box 6758, Harare

The following issues of *International Socialism* (second series) are available price £3 (including postage) from IS Journal, PO Box 82, London E3 3LH. *International Socialism* 2:58 and 2:65 are available on cassette from the Royal National Institute for the Blind (Peterborough Library Unit). Phone 01733 370777.

International Socialism 2:75 Summer 1997
John Rees: The class struggle under New Labour ★ Alex Callinicos: Europe: the mounting crisis ★ Lance Selfa: Mexico after the Zapatista uprising ★ William Keach: Rise like lions? Shelley and the revolutionary left ★ Judy Cox: What state are we really in? ★ John Parrington: In perspective: Valentin Voloshinov ★

International Socialism 2:74 Spring 1997
Colin Sparks: Tories, Labour and the crisis in education ★ Colin Wilson: The politics of information technology ★ Mike Gonzalez: No more heroes: Nicaragua 1996 ★ Christopher Hill: Tulmults and commotions: turning the world upside down ★ Peter Morgan: Capitalism without frontiers? ★ Alex Callinicos: Minds, machines and evolution ★ Anthony Arnove: In perspective: Noam Chomsky★

International Socialism 2:73 Winter 1996
Chris Harman: Globalisation: a critique of a new orthodoxy ★ Chris Bambery: Marxism and sport ★ John Parrington: Computers and consciousness: a reply to Alex Callinicos ★ Joe Faith: Dennett, materialism and empiricism ★ Megan Trudell: Who made the American Revolution? ★ Mark O'Brien: The class conflicts which shaped British history ★ John Newsinger: From class war to Cold War ★ Alex Callinicos: The state in debate ★ Charlie Kimber: Review article: coming to terms with barbarism in Rwanda in Burundi★

International Socialism 2:72 Autumn 1996
Alex Callinicos: Betrayal and discontent: Labour under Blair ★ Sue Cockerill and Colin Sparks: Japan in crisis ★ Richard Levins: When science fails us ★ Ian Birchall: The Babeuf bicentenary: conspiracy or revolutionary party? ★ Brian Manning: A voice for the poor ★ Paul O'Flinn: From the kingdom of necessity to the kingdom of freedom: Morris's *News from Nowhere* ★ Clare Fermont: Bookwatch: Palestine and the Middle East 'peace process'★

International Socialism 2:71 Summer 1996
Chris Harman: The crisis of bourgeois economics ★ Hassan Mahamdallie: William Morris and revolutionary Marxism ★ Alex Callinicos: Darwin, materialism and revolution ★ Chris Nineham: Raymond Williams: revitalising the left? ★ Paul Foot: A passionate prophet of liberation ★ Gill Hubbard: Why has feminism failed women? ★ Lee Sustar: Bookwatch: fighting to unite black and white★

International Socialism 2:70 Spring 1996
Alex Callinicos: South Africa after apartheid ★ Chris Harman: France's hot December ★ Brian Richardson: The making of a revolutionary ★ Gareth Jenkins: Why Lucky Jim turned right—an obituary of Kingsley Amis ★ Mark O'Brien: The bloody birth of capitalism ★ Lee Humber: Studies in revolution ★ Adrian Budd: A new life for Lenin ★ Martin Smith: Bookwatch: the General Strike★

International Socialism 2:69 Winter 1995
Lindsey German: The Balkan war: can there be peace? ★ Duncan Blackie: The left and the Balkan war ★ Nicolai Gentchev: The myth of welfare dependency ★ Judy Cox: Wealth, poverty and class in Britain today ★ Peter Morgan: Trade unions and strikes ★ Julie Waterson: The party at its peak ★ Megan Trudell: Living to some purpose ★ Nick Howard: The rise and fall of socialism in one city ★ Andy Durgan: Bookwatch: Civil war and revolution in Spain ★

International Socialism 2:68 Autumn 1995
Ruth Brown: Racism and immigration in Britain ★ John Molyneux: Is Marxism deterministic? ★ Stuart Hood: News from nowhere? ★ Lee Sustar: Communism in the heart of the beast ★ Peter Linebaugh: To the teeth and forehead of our faults ★ George Paizis: Back to the future ★ Phil Marshall: The children of stalinism ★ Paul D'Amato: Bookwatch: 100 years of cinema ★

International Socialism 2:67 Summer 1995
Paul Foot: When will the Blair bubble burst? ★ Chris Harman: From Bernstein to Blair—100 years

of revisionism ★ Chris Bambery: Was the Second World War a war for democracy? ★ Chris Nineham: Is the media all powerful? ★ Peter Morgan: How the West was won ★ Charlie Hore: Bookwatch: China since Mao ★

International Socialism 2:66 Spring 1995
Dave Crouch: The crisis in Russia and the rise of the right ★ Phil Gasper: Cruel and unusual punishment: the politics of crime in the United States ★ Alex Callinicos: Backwards to liberalism ★ John Newsinger: Matewan: film and working class struggle ★ John Rees: The light and the dark ★ Judy Cox: How to make the Tories disappear ★ Charlie Hore: Jazz: a reply to the critics ★ Pat Riordan: Bookwatch: Ireland ★

International Socialism 2:65 Special issue
Lindsey German: Frederick Engels: life of a revolutionary ★ John Rees: Engels' Marxism ★ Chris Harman: Engels and the origins of human society ★ Paul McGarr: Engels and natural science ★

International Socialism 2:64 Autumn 1994
Chris Harman: The prophet and the proletariat ★ Kieran Allen: What is changing in Ireland ★ Mike Haynes: The wrong road on Russia ★ Rob Ferguson: Hero and villain ★ Jane Elderton: Suffragette style ★ Chris Nineham: Two faces of modernism ★ Mike Hobart, Dave Harker and Matt Kelly: Three replies to 'Jazz—a people's music?' ★ Charlie Kimber: Bookwatch: South Africa—the struggle continues ★

International Socialism 2:63 Summer 1994
Alex Callinicos: Crisis and class struggle in Europe today ★ Duncan Blackie: The United Nations and the politics of imperialism ★ Brian Manning: The English Revolution and the transition from feudalism to capitalism ★ Lee Sustar: The roots of multi-racial labour unity in the United States ★ Peter Linebaugh: Days of villainy: a reply to two critics ★ Dave Sherry: Trotsky's last, greatest struggle ★ Peter Morgan: Geronimo and the end of the Indian wars ★ Dave Beecham: Ignazio Silone and *Fontamara* ★ Chris Bambery: Bookwatch: understanding fascism ★

International Socialism 2:62 Spring 1994
Sharon Smith: Mistaken identity—or can identity politics liberate the oppressed? ★ Iain Ferguson: Containing the crisis—crime and the Tories ★ John Newsinger: Orwell and the Spanish Revolution ★ Chris Harman: Change at the first millenium ★ Adrian Budd: Nation and empire—Labour's foreign policy 1945-51 ★ Gareth Jenkins: Novel questions ★ Judy Cox: Blake's revolution ★ Derek Howl: Bookwatch: the Russian Revolution ★

International Socialism 2:61 Winter 1994
Lindsey German: Before the flood? ★ John Molyneux: The 'politically correct' controversy ★ David McNally: E P Thompson—class struggle and historical materialism ★ Charlie Hore: Jazz—a people's music ★ Donny Gluckstein: Revolution and the challenge of labour ★ Charlie Kimber: Bookwatch: the Labour Party in decline ★

International Socialism 2:59 Summer 1993
Ann Rogers: Back to the workhouse ★ Kevin Corr and Andy Brown: The labour aristocracy and the roots of reformism ★ Brian Manning: God, Hill and Marx ★ Henry Maitles: Cutting the wire: a criticial appraisal of Primo Levi ★ Hazel Croft: Bookwatch: women and work ★

International Socialism 2:58 Spring 1993
Chris Harman: Where is capitalism going? (part one) ★ Ruth Brown and Peter Morgan: Politics and the class struggle today: a roundtable discussion ★ Richard Greeman: The return of Comrade Tulayev: Victor Serge and the tragic vision of Stalinism ★ Norah Carlin: A new English revolution ★ John Charlton: Building a new world ★ Colin Barker: A reply to Dave McNally ★

International Socialism 2:56 Autumn 1992
Chris Harman: The Return of the National Question ★ Dave Treece: Why the Earth Summit failed ★ Mike Gonzalez: Can Castro survive? ★ Lee Humber and John Rees: The good old cause—an interview with Christopher Hill ★ Ernest Mandel: The Impasse of Schematic Dogmatism ★

International Socialism 2:55 Summer 1992
Alex Callinicos: Race and class ★ Lee Sustar: Racism and class struggle in the American Civil War era ★ Lindsey German and Peter Morgan: Prospects for socialists—an interview with Tony Cliff ★ Robert Service: Did Lenin lead to Stalin? ★ Samuel Farber: In defence of democratic revolutionary socialism ★ David Finkel: Defending 'October' or sectarian dogmatism? ★ Robin Blackburn: Reply to John Rees ★ John Rees: Dedicated followers of fashion ★ Colin Barker: In praise of custom ★ Sheila McGregor: Revolutionary witness ★

International Socialism 2:54 Spring 1992
Sharon Smith: Twilight of the American dream ★ Mike Haynes: Class and crisis—the transition in eastern Europe ★ Costas Kossis: A miracle without end? Japanese capitalism and the world economy ★ Alex Callinicos: Capitalism and the state system: A reply to Nigel Harris ★ Steven Rose: Do animals have rights? ★ John Charlton: Crime and class in the 18th century ★ John Rees: Revolution, reform and working class culture ★ Chris Harman: Blood simple ★

International Socialism 2:51 Summer 1991
Chris Harman: The state and capitalism today ★ Alex Callinicos: The end of nationalism? ★ Sharon Smith: Feminists for a strong state? ★ Colin Sparks and Sue Cockerill: Goodbye to the Swedish miracle ★ Simon Phillips: The South African Communist Party and the South African working class ★ John Brown: Class conflict and the crisis of feudalism ★

International Socialism 2:49 Winter 1990
Chris Bambery: The decline of the Western Communist Parties ★ Ernest Mandel: A theory which has not withstood the test of time ★ Chris Harman: Criticism which does not withstand the test of logic ★ Derek Howl: The law of value In the USSR ★ Terry Eagleton: Shakespeare and the class struggle ★ Lionel Sims: Rape and pre-state societies ★ Sheila McGregor: A reply to Lionel Sims ★

International Socialism 2:48 Autumn 1990
Lindsey German: The last days of Thatcher ★ John Rees: The new imperialism ★ Neil Davidson and Donny Gluckstein: Nationalism and the class struggle in Scotland ★ Paul McGarr: Order out of chaos ★

International Socialism 2:46 Winter 1989
Chris Harman: The storm breaks ★ Alex Callinicos: Can South Africa be reformed? ★ John Saville: Britain, the Marshall Plan and the Cold War ★ Sue Clegg: Against the stream ★ John Rees: The rising bourgeoisie ★

International Socialism 2:44 Autumn 1989
Charlie Hore: China: Tiananmen Square and after ★ Sue Clegg: Thatcher and the welfare state ★ John Molyneux: *Animal Farm* revisited ★ David Finkel: After Arias, is the revolution over? ★ John Rose: Jews in Poland ★

International Socialism 2:43 Summer 1989 (Reprint—special price £4.50)
Marxism and the Great French Revolution by Paul McGarr and Alex Callinicos

International Socialism 2:42 Spring 1989
Chris Harman: The myth of market socialism ★ Norah Carlin: Roots of gay oppression ★ Duncan Blackie: Revolution in science ★ International Socialism Index ★

International Socialism 2:41 Winter 1988
Polish socialists speak out: Solidarity at the Crossroads ★ Mike Haynes: Nightmares of the market ★ Jack Robertson: Socialists and the unions ★ Andy Strouthous: Are the unions in decline? ★ Richard Bradbury: What is Post-Structuralism? ★ Colin Sparks: George Bernard Shaw ★

International Socialism 2:39 Summer 1988
Chris Harman and Andy Zebrowski: Glasnost, before the storm ★ Chanie Rosenberg: Labour and the fight against fascism ★ Mike Gonzalez: Central America after the Peace Plan ★ Ian Birchall: Raymond Williams ★ Alex Callinicos: Reply to John Rees ★

International Socialism 2:35 Summer 1987
Pete Green: Capitalism and the Thatcher years ★ Alex Callinicos: Imperialism, capitalism and the state today ★ Ian Birchall: Five years of *New Socialist* ★ Callinicos and Wood debate 'Looking for alternatives to reformism' ★ David Widgery replies on 'Beating Time' ★

International Socialism 2:31 Winter 1985
Alex Callinicos: Marxism and revolution in South Africa ★ Tony Cliff: The tragedy of A J Cook ★ Nigel Harris: What to do with London? The strategies of the GLC ★

International Socialism 2:30 Autumn 1985
Gareth Jenkins: Where is the Labour Party heading? ★ David McNally: Debt, inflation and the rate of profit ★ Ian Birchall: The terminal crisis in the British Communist Party ★ replies on Women's oppression and *Marxism Today* ★